Grammar Galaxy

Adventures in Language Arts

Protostar

Melanie Wilson, Ph.D.
Rebecca Mueller, Illustrator

Dedicated to future guardians of Grammar Galaxy.

Table of Contents

A Note to Teachers 1

Prologue 2

Unit I: Adventures in Literature 3

Chapter 1: Book Reports 4

Chapter 2: Classics 10

Chapter 3: Myths 15

Chapter 4: Fables 19

Chapter 5: Autobiographies 23

Chapter 6: Alliteration 28

Chapter 7: Story Action 33

Chapter 8: Drama Terms 39

Unit II: Adventures in Spelling & Vocabulary 44

Chapter 9: Homophones 45

Chapter 10: Acronyms 51

Chapter 11: Root Words 56

Chapter 12: Idioms 61

Chapter 13: Dictionary Skills 65

Chapter 14: Spelling Rules 70

Unit III: Adventures in Grammar 76

Chapter 15: Possessive Nouns & Pronouns 77

Chapter 16: Helping Verbs 82

Chapter 17: Verb Tenses 87

Chapter 18: Irregular Verbs 94

Chapter 19: Linking Verbs 98

Chapter 20: Prepositions 103

Chapter 21: Parts of Speech 107

Chapter 22: Subjects 112

Chapter 23: Predicates 117

Chapter 24: Compound Subjects & Predicates 121

Chapter 25: Commas 125

Unit IV: Adventures in Composition & Speaking 131

Chapter 26: Copywork 132

Chapter 27: Combining Short Sentences 138

Chapter 28: Sentences & Fragments 143

Chapter 29: Paragraphs 148

Chapter 30: Word Order 153

Chapter 31: Story Completion 157

Chapter 32: Encyclopedias 162

Chapter 33: Shape Poems 167

Chapter 34: Friendly Letters 174

Chapter 35: Keyboarding 180

Chapter 36: Keywords 185

About the Author 191

About the Illustrator 192

A Note to Teachers

I'm passionate about language arts. I love to read, write, and speak. As a homeschooling mom, I wanted my own children and my friends' children to share my passion. Over the years, I found aspects of many different curricula that clicked with my students. But I never found something that did everything I wanted a complete curriculum for elementary students to do:

- Use the most powerful medium to teach language arts: story
- Give the why of language arts to motivate students
- Teach to mastery rather than drill the same concepts year after year
- Limit seat work and use little-to-no-prep games to teach instead
- Teach literary concepts, vocabulary, spelling, writing & speaking

I felt called to create my own fast, easy, and fun curriculum for homeschooling parents and others who want to see students succeed in language arts.

Grammar Galaxy: Protostar is for students who are beginning readers and writers at about a third-grade level. They should have used separate phonics and handwriting curriculum. And they should have completed *Grammar Galaxy: Nebula* or its equivalent. *Protostar* should be read to students unless they and their teachers are confident they can read and comprehend the stories and mission instructions on their own. The stories and concepts are appropriate for students in first to sixth grade, however, making this a perfect read-aloud for families. Be sure to point out the synonyms for vocabulary words that are provided. Following each story, there are questions to check for understanding. With your help, the student should complete the corresponding mission in the *Mission Manual* before moving on to the next story. The *Mission Manual* can be purchased at GrammarGalaxyBooks.com/shop.

My hope is that your student will accept the call to be a guardian of Grammar Galaxy.

Melanie Wilson

Prologue

The king of Grammar Galaxy stood in the observatory, pondering the events of the previous year. He had been wise to make his children, Kirk, Luke, and Ellen English, official guardians of the galaxy. They had done well in protecting the English language from the Gremlin. The other young guardians of the galaxy had done their part by completing assigned missions.

Despite the Gremlin's evil plans, children were reading, words were where they belonged on the various planets, and young people were learning to write and speak well. The king was pleased, but he was also worried.

He paced back and forth, wondering how the Gremlin would try to destroy the English language next. The king hoped the guardians would remain strong enough to defeat him.

Unit I: Adventures in Literature

Chapter 1

The royal family sat around the breakfast table. The king reminded them of the upcoming book report deadline. He explained that, for the first time, their book reports would be shared across the galaxy. They would be giving them **orally,** rather than submitting them in written form.

★ ★ ★ ★ ★ ★ ★ ★ ★ ★

orally – *out loud*

★ ★ ★ ★ ★ ★ ★ ★ ★ ★

Ellen chattered excitedly with her mother, asking her what she thought they should wear. Kirk said he was going to have trouble choosing a book because he had read so many amazing titles.

Everyone left the table stating their intention to get to work immediately, except Luke. Luke went to his bedchamber and took out his reading calendars. He had marked stars to show he had read, but he didn't have the titles of the books he'd read.

He sat on his bed trying to recall his favorite titles of the last year, with no luck. Then he realized he could just look on his bookshelves. He spent time flipping through the pages of some of the books. He smiled as he recalled his favorite characters and plots. He was relieved as he realized he would easily be able to choose one of the books for his report.

He figured he had plenty of time to have a snack. Luke made his way to the kitchen where he asked Cook if she had anything especially tasty for him. She **complied** and **presented** Luke with freshly baked cookies. After his snack, Luke decided to take Comet for a long walk.

★ ★ ★ ★ ★ ★ ★ ★ ★ ★

complied – *obeyed*

presented – *gave*

★ ★ ★ ★ ★ ★ ★ ★ ★ ★

At dinner that evening everyone chatted about the book they had chosen for their report. Luke smiled and stated that he had his selection narrowed down to three books. The king smiled approvingly. "That's excellent, Luke. I look forward to hearing your report."

In the days that followed, Luke figured he still had plenty of time to finish his report. One of his three favorite books was part of a series. He was excited to read the next book, so he checked it out of the library. He starting reading it and also kept busy doing math and science.

A week later when Ellen asked him about his report, Luke realized that he had to get started. He sat down in his bedchamber one evening with paper and pencil. First, he wrote the titles of the three books he had chosen. *Which is my favorite?* he wondered. When he couldn't decide, he asked Comet to sniff one. But Comet barely raised an eyebrow. Luke sighed. "Okay. I'm tired, too. I'll decide tomorrow."

The next several days were full of activities for Luke. He did think about his report but told himself he could finish it in an hour or two. He had a sick feeling in his stomach when he awoke two days before he was supposed to be giving his report. "I have to get this done!" he declared.

After a full breakfast, he returned to his room. He was determined to choose a book. "I know! I'll choose the first book in the series I'm reading." He was proud of himself for deciding. He would have plenty of time to organize a game of spaceball with his friends when he was done with the report.

On a new sheet of paper, he wrote the book title. He smiled as he imagined himself announcing the book. Then his smile faded. "Now what am I supposed to say? I don't know even know how to write a book report!" He felt sick again as he thought of millions of people watching him. He felt even sicker as he thought of telling his family that he hadn't started his report. "What should I do?" he asked Comet, who seemed just as sleepy as he had days before.

"I know! I'm really not feeling well. There's no way I can write this report anyway. I need to rest. Right, boy?" Comet groaned as he tried to get back to sleep. "You're not feeling well, either. I can't help it that I'm sick."

Luke climbed into bed and imagined himself having to do his report. It helped him to feel sick. Then he used his communicator to contact his mother. "Mother," he said weakly. "I'm not well."

"Oh, no!" she cried. "What's wrong?"

"I don't know. I feel sick."

"What can I bring you? Do you have a fever? Should I call the doctor?"

"No, no fever. I don't need anything. I'll be fine. Well, maybe some soup would be good. And crackers. I could try some pudding, too. Chocolate milk would taste good."

"Okay, dear. I'll ask Cook to make up a tray and I'll bring it to you."

"I don't want you to get sick, too. Just have someone leave it by the door." This worried the queen even more, but she was proud of Luke for thinking of her. "Oh, and Mother?" Luke said.

"Yes, sweet Luke?"

"I'm so disappointed, but I don't think I'll be able to do the book report tomorrow."

"Oh, goodness, Luke. Don't worry about that. You'll probably be fine by tomorrow anyway."

Luke felt quite guilty when he got the "Get Well Soon" note on his meal tray. But when he thought about telling everyone the truth, he really did feel sick. He tried to pass the time by reading more of his new book. But that made him feel sick, too. When he finally fell asleep, he had repeated nightmares about the book report.

He woke up to his mother knocking gently on the door. "Luke, how are you?" she called.

Before he could think, he answered, "I'm fine!" When he remembered, he called out, "Uh, I'm starting to feel sick, though."

The queen came in and held a hand to Luke's forehead. "No fever," she announced. She looked at the empty food dishes on the tray from the night before. "Appetite seems okay, too."

Luke interjected, "I don't think I'm well enough to do the book report." He held his breath, waiting for his mother to agree.

"I see," she said. She went to Luke's desk and picked up the papers lying there. "Is this your report?"

"Yes...no. That's just the title," he stammered.

"Where's the finished report then?" she asked, staring at him until he could stand it no more.

"Okay, I admit it! I'm not sick. I don't have my report done. I don't even know how to write a book report. I waited so long to start it and then I was too scared to tell you. I'm so sorry! Really I am. Please forgive me, Mother. Please?" Luke's eyes welled up with tears. He jumped out of bed and ran to her, hugging her tightly.

His mother sighed and crouched down to look into Luke's eyes. "I'm disappointed that you lied. We were all worried about you," she said.

"I know. I feel so guilty!"

"I can see that you do. You should. The next time you're really sick we may not believe you."

"I know. I won't lie again."

"You will need to apologize to Cook and the rest of the family."

Luke sighed. "I will."

"And you will have to give your report."

"I'll make a fool of myself! I don't know how to write a book report," he wailed.

The queen smiled. "In the excitement of getting ready to read our reports on TV, I forgot that you hadn't written one before. Get dressed. You can apologize to everyone at breakfast. Then we'll get to work on your report."

Luke was nervous about admitting he had lied. But it was better than having to go on television without a report.

Luke was relieved when he told Cook and his family that he'd lied and they forgave him. He thought his punishment made sense. He would help Cook make dinner for the family and would help clean up, too.

The queen explained that Luke hadn't been taught how to write a book report. So the king called for the guidebook. He read the entry for them.

Book Reports
A book report is a way for readers to think about and share what they've read. Book reports develop literature, writing, and speaking skills. Beginning book reports include an introduction. The introduction gives the book title and author as well as the reason for choosing the book. The body, or main part of the book report, should describe the setting, characters, and plot. The conclusion, or ending, should give the reader's opinion and what was learned. Book reports can include illustrations. They can be written or presented orally.

"I remember what the setting, characters, and plot of a book are," Luke said confidently.

"Me, too," Ellen said. "The setting is where and when the book happens. It's also the mood."

"Right, like scary or funny," Luke added.

"The characters are the people in the story. But sometimes animals are the characters," Ellen continued.

"The plot is the problem that is solved in the story," Kirk said.

"I remember this," Luke said. "But I have to be honest and say that I don't remember everything you said should be in the book report."

"I can help," the queen said. She showed Luke some forms that he could use to write his report.

"Wow! If I had these a few weeks ago, I could have written my report easy," Luke said.

"Easily," his mother corrected.

"Mother, do you think anyone else waited to write their book report at the last minute? I mean, do you think there are other kids who don't know how to write reports?" Luke asked.

The queen smiled. "Are you saying what I think you're saying?" Luke grinned.

"Luke, you get to work on your book report. Ellen and I will send out a mission to our fellow guardians called Book Reports. We wouldn't want anyone else to get the Book Report Flu," Kirk said. Everyone laughed.

What does *complied* mean?

What should Luke have done instead of pretending to be sick?

What should be included in the introduction to your book report?

Chapter 2

"What are you reading, Luke?" the king asked. He was pleased to see his son reading on a rainy Saturday afternoon.

"*The Invaders*," Luke answered. When his father didn't seem to know the title, he explained, "It's really cool. These aliens land on our planet. They multiply by attaching themselves to people like leeches. They try to take over the planet."

The king **grimaced**. "I see." He stroked his beard. "You know what I thought was really cool at your age? *Charlotte's Web*."

★ ★ ★ ★ ★ ★ ★ ★ ★ ★

grimaced – *frowned*

★ ★ ★ ★ ★ ★ ★ ★ ★ ★

"Ooh, is it about spider aliens?" Luke asked.

"No, no aliens. But it is about a spider."

"No aliens and it's cool?" Luke asked doubtfully.

"Definitely! It's about a spelling spider."

"A spider that spells? It doesn't sound cool. It sounds like a lesson book."

"Oh, no. It's not about spelling," the king started to explain.

"But you just said it was!" Luke protested.

"Well, the spider does spell, but that's not the point of the story." When Luke continued to look confused, the king said he had an idea. "Let's check *Charlotte's Web* out from the library."

"But I'm reading *Invaders*."

"I know. We could read *Charlotte's Web* out loud as a family. That would be wonderful!"

Luke didn't seem to share his father's enthusiasm, but the king was determined. "Screen," he ordered. "Please put *Charlotte's Web* on hold at the library's main branch."

"Certainly, Your Majesty," Screen answered. A description of the book appeared on the screen, but the book cover was missing. A moment later, Screen reported, "I'm afraid that title cannot be checked out, Your Majesty."

10

"You mean all copies of *Charlotte's Web* are checked out?" the king asked, beaming. He smiled at Luke as if to say he was right in suggesting a great book.

"No, Your Majesty. There are no copies available in the library's main branch."

"That's strange. Check the other branches then."

Screen immediately gave the king the news. There were no copies available for checking out in the entire library system.

"This makes no sense!" the king cried. "This book is a classic. Where have all the copies gone?"

Screen responded by displaying a news video. A female reporter stood in front of what looked like a warehouse. Books were being carted into the entrance.

"I'm here at the Long-Term Care Library where classic books are being moved. Here they will receive the care they need. They will not be checked out and risk being damaged. This move is part of the Classic Care Initiative. To find out how you can get involved in caring for classic books, go to ClassicCare.org. All funds will go to caring for these classic books," the reporter explained.

"Long-Term Care Library? That's just an old storage building. Those books are being brought there to die!" The king was **indignant**. "Who authorized this? It's an outrage!"

★ ★ ★ ★ ★ ★ ★ ★ ★ ★

indignant – *angry*

★ ★ ★ ★ ★ ★ ★ ★ ★ ★

Luke hadn't seen his father so upset since the Gremlin got kids to stop reading. "Father, isn't it a good idea to take care of old books so they don't fall apart?"

"All books should be cared for, Luke. But books are made to be read, not warehoused!" he roared. The king paced. "I have to find out who started the Classic Care Initiative." As he was about to order Screen to look up the website, he stopped. "I know who's behind this. The Gremlin! If he can get people to stop reading the classics, he can destroy the galaxy."

Luke appeared unconvinced. "If people don't read old books, the galaxy will be destroyed? A book about a spelling spider doesn't seem as important as the book *Invaders*. Spiders don't spell, but aliens could really overtake our planet."

His father started to answer but stopped himself. "I need to tell Kirk and Ellen, too. Let's find them." Luke and Comet, fresh from a nap, followed the king.

11

When the king found his other two children, he asked them to join him in the castle library. He explained to Kirk and Ellen what had been happening. Then he removed *The Guide to Grammar Galaxy* from a shelf. He looked up classics in the table of contents, and read the entry.

Classics
A classic is a great book that has long-lasting appeal to many readers. Classics are often studied and quoted. The definition of a classic book is often debated. A few popular children's classics are listed here.

A Bear Called Paddington	A Wrinkle in Time
The Adventures of Tom Sawyer	Alice's Adventures in Wonderland
Anne of Green Gables series	Black Beauty
Bridge to Terabithia	The Cat in the Hat
Charlie and the Chocolate Factory	The Chronicles of Narnia series
The Giving Tree	Green Eggs & Ham
Heidi	The Hobbit
Little House series	The Little Prince
Little Women	Mary Poppins
No, David	Peter Pan
Pippi Longstocking	Treasure Island
The Tale of Peter Rabbit	Where the Wild Things Are
The Very Hungry Caterpillar	The Wonderful Wizard of Oz
Winnie-the-Pooh	

"I've read some of those books," Ellen said.

"As well you should have," the king answered. "Unfortunately, you won't be able to read any more of them. They've been moved to the Long-Term Care Library. No one can check them out."

"How old does a book have to be to be a classic?" Kirk asked.

"There's no agreement on that. There are classics like *No, David!* that aren't that old. That's why it makes no sense to put classics in storage. Many classics have recently been reprinted. They don't need to be protected; they need to be read," the king answered **emphatically**.

"What can we do to get them out of storage?" Kirk asked.

"I'm going to talk to the head librarian," the king said. He asked Screen to contact her immediately. When she appeared on screen, the king explained what had happened to their classic books.

★ ★ ★ ★ ★ ★ ★ ★ ★ ★

emphatically – *definitely*

★ ★ ★ ★ ★ ★ ★ ★ ★ ★

"Oh, I know," the librarian answered.

The king was surprised. "You know? Why didn't you contact me?"

"I thought you approved of the Classic Care Initiative. I want to protect copies of old books. But that wasn't the main reason I liked the plan. The truth is, people haven't been checking the classics out."

The king was astonished. "Have kids stopped reading again?"

"Oh, no, they're reading," she reassured him. "They're just reading popular fiction instead of the classics."

"Like *Invaders*?" Luke asked.

The librarian smiled. "Yes, Luke, like *Invaders*."

"This is terrible news!" the king declared. When his three children seemed confused, he explained. "Reading classics increases our vocabulary. And you remember how important it is to know lots of words, right?" The children nodded. "When people talk about these classic books, we will understand. Luke, remember when you didn't know that *Charlotte's Web* wasn't about spelling?" Luke nodded again. "Reading classics is also a great way to learn about our history. Many stories are set in the past, so we learn about what life was like many years ago."

"Right! Like Laura Ingalls Wilder," Ellen added.

"Exactly!" the king answered. Beyond that, classic books are like old friends. We don't want to put them in a warehouse and forget about them. We want to reread them and share them with others who would enjoy them. Just like *Charlotte's Web*. I want to share this classic with you. But there are no copies of it to check out now."

"Can't you order all the classic books to be returned to the library branches that they came from?" Kirk asked.

"I sure can," the king smiled. "And I will. But that won't solve the problem."

"Because kids aren't reading them, right, Father?" Luke asked.

The king put his arm around Luke's shoulder. "You've got it, Luke. As Guardians of the Galaxy, you have to devise a plan for getting people to read classic books. If you don't, I'm afraid the classics will end up back in a warehouse."

13

Kirk, Luke, and Ellen brainstormed ideas. When they had chosen the best ideas, they sent them out as a mission to their fellow guardians. They called the mission Classics.

What does *emphatically* mean?

What is a classic book?

Have you read any of the classics listed in the guidebook?

Chapter 3

The children found their parents obviously upset at the breakfast table one morning. The queen was pointing out something in a newspaper they hadn't seen before.

"They're suggesting you're dangerous to the galaxy!" she cried. Her face flushed with anger.

"Dear, this is just the *Galactic Enquirer*. No one takes this paper seriously," the king said.

"Why was Cook reading it then?" the queen asked. "It will be the talk of the planet! I know all my friends will read it and will wonder if it's true."

"Wonder if what's true?" Luke asked.

The queen looked to the king for permission to tell him and he nodded. "The *Galactic Enquirer* says your father is a descendant of the god who created Grammar Galaxy."

The kids laughed. "Father is an amazing king, but a god? That's just silly," Kirk chuckled.

"I think it's cool!" Luke cried. "You're like Hercules, Father." Luke put his hands on his hips and puffed out his chest to look strong.

It was the king's turn to chuckle. "Don't you remember what happened when my biography was written like a tall tale? I was really strong then." The king flexed his bicep. "But once you children found the parts that were exaggerated, I was back to normal."

"The other guardians helped, too," Ellen added.

"Oh, yes. I wouldn't be my normal self without them. Though it was pretty fun while it lasted." The king laughed, but noticed that the queen was still upset. "Why are you fretting over this, dear?"

"Have you read the whole thing? Let me read it to you and maybe you'll be as concerned as I am."

King of Grammar Galaxy Could Destroy Us All

An ancient document has been discovered that reveals the origins of our galaxy. In the beginning, everyone lived peaceably together on one planet. We were ruled by a god-king named Grammar. All was well until the Gremlin issued a challenge. He challenged Grammar and his brother Math, the god-king of Math Galaxy, to a contest.

 The brother who could solve a riddle would prove that his galaxy was more important.

The riddle **perplexed** Grammar. After days of trying to solve it, he admitted to the Gremlin that he didn't have the answer. His brother, Math, answered the Gremlin easily and was proclaimed the winner.

Grammar was so angry that he had been bested by his brother that he squeezed the English planet. He squeezed it with so much force that it exploded, creating all the smaller planets in our galaxy today.

Some historians believe Grammar was **duped** because the Gremlin gave Math the answer to the riddle. Either way, we English citizens are left with a question. The Gremlin is still up to his dirty tricks. Our king does his best to protect us. But should we be more afraid of our king than our old rival? After all, it was our king's ancestor whose rage resulted in the **fractured** galaxy we have today. What if the Gremlin is able to create another fit of rage?

The king laughed again when she finished reading. "How can you laugh?" The queen was astonished.

"Because it's ridiculous to think that I could destroy the galaxy or that I would. I'm not a god, dear."

"I know that, but the people of Grammar Galaxy may not know that. And you do have a temper."

The king sighed. "All right, I'll handle this so you won't worry."

"Are you going to make the paper admit that they lied?"

"No. Some people would think I was threatening the paper to cover up the truth."

The queen had to admit that he was right. Before she could ask him about his plan, he asked for the guidebook to be brought to him. When it arrived, he addressed the children. "What the *Galactic Enquirer* printed is a myth." He then read from the guidebook.

★ ★ ★ ★ ★ ★ ★ ★ ★ ★ ★

perplexed – *confused*

duped – *tricked*

fractured – *split*

★ ★ ★ ★ ★ ★ ★ ★ ★ ★ ★

Myths
Myths are the oldest form of fictional stories. They have been told and passed down to explain creation or natural events. The main characters are gods or people with supernatural powers. Prometheus's gift of fire to people is an example of a myth. Myths are not based on real people or events.

"Does that mean there was never a god-king of Grammar Galaxy?" Ellen asked.

"That's right, Ellen. There have been kings before me, but none of them have been gods," the king answered.

"My question is, who's Prometheus?" Luke asked.

"That's a good question, Luke. I'll tell you the story."

Everyone sat down to listen to the king.

"Prometheus was one of the sons of the god, Zeus. He didn't enjoy living on Mount Olympus, where the rest of the gods lived. So he went to live with people instead. After living with them for a while, he noticed that they were unhappy. They didn't have fire for light, warmth, or cooking. So he went to his father and asked if he would share his fire with them. His father refused. Zeus was afraid that if people had fire they could become more powerful than the gods. That

17

didn't stop Prometheus. He knew people would be so much happier with fire and he wanted to help them. He stole fire from his father and gave it to the people. When Zeus learned what he had done, he was angry. He had Prometheus chained to the side of a mountain to suffer forever. Prometheus was rescued, but that's another story."

"Wow! So that's how we got fire? That was very brave and kind of Prometheus," Luke said.

"Luke, this is a myth, remember?" Kirk said.

"That's right, Luke. What makes this story a myth?" the king asked.

"Well, it's an old story that's been told a lot. And it explains how we got fire."

"Yes. What else?"

"It has gods in it."

"It does. Is it based on real people or events? Did Prometheus really give us fire?"

"I guess not. But it would be really cool if he did."

The king laughed. "That's one of the reasons people believe myths. It would be kind of fun to think they were true."

"I don't think anyone would think you destroying the galaxy would be fun," the queen interjected.

"Dear, please don't worry. I'm going to have the children send out a mission to the guardians. If they complete their mission successfully, no one will believe the article."

The king worked with Kirk, Luke, and Ellen on a mission called Myths. He then suggested that they reassure Cook that he was not a god, even though he did have a temper.

What does *duped* mean?

Why was the queen upset about the newspaper article?

What makes the article about the king a myth?

Chapter 4

One evening after dinner, the king asked the children if they had been reading to build character. When they seemed confused, he explained that reading wasn't just for entertainment and information. "There are books that can help us develop honorable qualities," he said.

The king had an idea and requested that the book *Aesop's Fables* be brought from the castle library. He handed it to Luke and suggested that he choose one of the short stories in the book to read.

"A-e-soap's Fables?" Luke read.

The king chuckled. "It's pronounced E-sop's Fables, Luke."

Luke nodded and paged through the book until he found a story that looked interesting and read aloud.

THE WOLF IN SHEEP'S CLOTHING

A Wolf found great difficulty in getting at the sheep, owing to the **vigilance** of the shepherd and his dogs. But one day it found the skin

★ ★ ★ ★ ★ ★ ★ ★ ★ ★

vigilance – *watching*

★ ★ ★ ★ ★ ★ ★ ★ ★ ★

of a sheep that had been killed and thrown aside. So it put the skin on over its own pelt and strolled down among the sheep. An orphaned lamb began to follow the Wolf in the Sheep's clothing. So leading the lamb a little apart, the wolf soon made a meal of her. For some time he succeeded in **deceiving** the sheep and enjoying **hearty** meals.

★ ★ ★ ★ ★ ★ ★ ★ ★ ★

deceiving – *tricking*

hearty – *full*

★ ★ ★ ★ ★ ★ ★ ★ ★ ★

"That's awful!" Ellen cried.

The queen held her arms out to Ellen and she went to her.

"It's just a story, El," Kirk reassured her.

"Yes, it's just a story, but Luke left out the most important part. Luke, read the moral," the king said.

"The moral?"

"Yes, yes, the moral. It will give us the lesson to be learned," the king explained.

"There's nothing here," Luke said, scanning the page.

"What? Let me see," the king said. He took the book from Luke and could not immediately find the moral, either. He paged through the book and after some time, appeared to be very upset. "There are no morals listed anywhere in this book!"

"Were they always there, dear? It's been ages since we read fables," the queen said.

"Fables have morals. They've always had them!" The king was losing his temper quickly. The queen nodded, hoping to calm him down. The king asked a servant to bring him the guidebook so he could prove himself correct. When it arrived, he read the entry on fables for the family.

Fables

A fable is a short story, usually including animals as characters. The story is used to teach a lesson, which is called the moral of a story. The moral is often given at the end of the story. *Aesop's Fables* are the collected tales of an ancient Greek storyteller. Hundreds of fables are said to be Aesop's fables. But many of them were told by others living around the world.

"So there's a lesson in 'A Wolf in Sheep's Clothing'?" Luke asked.

"Right. But it's missing," the king said. He asked Screen to do a search of recent news stories having to do with morals or fables.

"I believe this is what you're looking for, Your Majesty," Screen replied. A replay of a news story began. A reporter stood in front of a group of protesters. They carried signs that said "No morals" and "My morals are my business."

"These men and women are upset about the morals included in books. They say they have the right to have their own beliefs," the reporter said.

"That's right! Stay out of my business!" a man interrupted, yelling at the camera.

The reporter nervously passed the newscast back to the anchor.

Screen then displayed live footage on planet Composition. A warehouse was filled with people who were busy screening books and websites. Occasionally someone would call out, "Moral removed!" The rest of the screeners would cheer. The king had Screen zoom in on a large banner inside the building. It read, "Proud to be a Moral-Free Facility."

The king was shocked. "Who authorized this? What a waste of time! Does no one understand that a moral is a valuable lesson?" The king continued talking to himself until Kirk asked him if they could help.

"Help? Oh, yes. You can help. I'm just so stunned by this. I never saw it coming. The Gremlin has obviously tricked people into believing that morals limit their freedom. The truth is that learning morals from fables can protect us. We can learn from stories instead of experience. We learn character, too. No wonder the Gremlin wanted to get rid of morals."

"How can we get the morals back, Father?" Ellen asked.

"I'm not sure we *can* get them back," her father said.

The queen was shocked to hear him sound so defeated. "There's nothing that can be done?" she asked.

"I didn't say that. I don't know if we can get all the morals back. I think we can recover some of them from recycling. We'll have to rewrite the rest. One thing I can definitely do is have this silly facility shut down immediately!" The king was ready to use his communicator to get started when Luke stopped him.

"How are we going to get the morals back to their fables?" Luke asked.

21

The king smiled for the first time since discovering the missing morals. "That will be a job for you three. Kirk, you'll have to get to planet Composition immediately. Pick up all the morals you find and copy everything put in digital recycling."

"I know that we can probably match morals to fables, but you said something about writing morals. How will we know what the moral of a story is?" Luke asked.

"You'll have to think about what lesson a fable teaches. I know you can do it," the king said. Luke didn't look so sure. But he ran to the spaceporter with his brother and sister, hoping his father was right.

When the English children arrived on planet Composition, the king's officers were already clearing the building. Luke was excited when he found what he was sure was the moral for "A Wolf in Sheep's Clothing." He read it to his brother and sister. "'Appearances can be deceiving.' That means things aren't always what they seem, right?" Kirk and Ellen agreed that it was likely the missing moral.

After a few hours collecting more morals and stories, the three were overwhelmed. In order to return the morals, they would have to read hundreds of fables.

"This is going to take forever!" Luke wailed. Kirk had to agree. Ellen pointed out that the guardians could benefit from character building, too. They connected with Screen via communicator. They asked for help sending a mission called Fables.

What does *vigilance* mean?

What kind of characters do fables usually have?

What was the moral of "A Wolf in Sheep's Clothing"?

22

Chapter 5

The queen found her husband in his study. He was reading his biography and frowning.

"What's wrong, dear?" the queen asked. "I thought your biography was fixed."

"It's not a tall tale anymore," the king said, sighing. "But it doesn't describe the real me. I was hoping that my biographer would have included more about my years growing up and also about you." The king stood and hugged his wife.

"But, dear, this is your biography. It's not my story. Can you ask your biographer to rewrite it again?" the queen asked.

"No, I can't. He was upset when I asked him to take out all the parts about how smart and strong and generous I am. Now that I think of it, that's another problem. This version makes it sound like I'm not smart or strong or generous at all."

"Does it matter? I mean, we all know the real you. You're an amazing husband, father, and ruler." It was the queen's turn to hug her husband.

"Thank you, my dear."

Days passed and the king continued to seem unhappy. The children noticed and asked their mother about it. She explained that he was dissatisfied with his biography. Kirk suggested that he request another rewrite. The queen repeated what the king had said: It wasn't an option.

Ellen was in the castle library when she saw her father walking by himself in the garden. It bothered her so much to see her father so **dispirited**. She wondered if there were a way to fix her father's biography. She took the guidebook from the shelf and looked up biographies.

★ ★ ★ ★ ★ ★ ★ ★ ★ ★

dispirited – *unhappy*

★ ★ ★ ★ ★ ★ ★ ★ ★ ★

Biography
Bio is a Greek word root meaning "life." *Graph* is a Greek word root meaning "to write." A biography is the story of a person's life written by someone else. It is written in third person, using the pronouns *he* or *she*. A biography requires a lot of research and will include facts and opinions. Biographies are usually written in chronological order. Earliest events, like the person's childhood, are described first. A biography may, however, describe just one period in a person's life. *See also:* **Autobiography**

"What's an autobiography?" she asked out loud. She decided to look that up, too.

Autobiography

Autos is a Greek word root meaning "self." An autobiography is a life story you write yourself. Autobiographies are written in first person, using the pronoun *I*. The story relies less on research and more on the author's memory. Like biographies, autobiographies are usually written in chronological order. Earlier events are described first. An autobiography may cover only one period of a person's life.

There is a trick to remember the difference between an autobiography and a biography. A biography is a life story written by someone else. Think of an auto as a car you drive yourself. Think of a bus (which begins with b like biography) as a vehicle someone else drives.

"That's it! Father needs to write his own life story." She skipped out of the library, eager to tell him. She hoped he would cheer up.

Ellen explained to her father that he could write an autobiography. Then he could have his life story be exactly what he wanted. His **countenance** brightened immediately.

★ ★ ★ ★ ★ ★ ★ ★ ★ ★

countenance – *face*

★ ★ ★ ★ ★ ★ ★ ★ ★ ★

"Write my own book?"

"Yes! It would be wonderful. I know you're a great writer."

"Well, thank you, Ellen. I'm going to have to think about this." But Ellen noted that her father looked happier than he had in ages.

The next day at breakfast, the king had an announcement. Thanks to Ellen, he said, he had decided to write his autobiography. Ellen explained the difference between an autobiography and a biography to Luke. "Father's going to drive his own life story!" he exclaimed.

Ellen laughed. "Sort of."

The king shared his excitement to get started. He excused himself from the table and went to his study.

That evening at dinner, everyone took turns asking the king how the writing had gone. He muttered something about making notes and needing an outline. This pattern of asking and the king putting his family off continued for a week. Finally, he admitted he wasn't making any progress.

"Writing my autobiography is harder than I thought," the king said **meekly**.

★ ★ ★ ★ ★ ★ ★ ★ ★ ★

meekly – *humbly*

★ ★ ★ ★ ★ ★ ★ ★ ★ ★

His family reassured him that he would be able to finish the book. But he persisted. "I appreciate your support, but I think I need help."

His family was surprised by this humble admission. "Is there any way we can help you?" Ellen asked sweetly.

"You've been helping by asking me about my progress. The kind of help I need is a ghostwriter."

"A ghostwriter? Will your autobiography have scary stories in it?" Luke asked.

The king laughed. "No, Luke. Although some of the problems I've had with the Gremlin have been pretty scary. A ghostwriter is someone who helps you write a book but isn't listed as an author. They're called ghostwriters because you don't see their names on the book."

For several months the king worked with a ghostwriter on his autobiography. The family didn't see much of him. Luke said he thought their father was a ghostwriter, too, because he seemed to have disappeared. The queen urged everyone to have patience because it was such an important project.

Finally, the king announced it was finished. "But I'm not going to publish it."

"What?!" his family exclaimed in shock.

In response to their many questions, the king explained. "If I publish this book, I'll be really smart and strong and generous again. The guardians would have to look for all the parts of the book that are exaggerated."

"You mean it's a tall tale again?" Luke asked.

"Yes." The king looked embarrassed. "I thought my ghostwriter could help, but he didn't want to tell me that what I said was unbelievable."

"So now what are you going to do?" Ellen asked.

"I've decided to rewrite my autobiography for my family. I don't have to publish it. But I want you to have it to keep."

The queen was delighted. "What a wonderful idea!"

"Father, I learned something that I think could help," Ellen said. When her father asked her what she meant, she explained. "The guidebook said an autobiography could be about just part of your life."

"That's true!" the king said, stroking his beard. "I could start by writing about the worst battles I've had with the Gremlin."

"Yeah!" Luke exclaimed.

"Or I could write about how I met your mother," he said, kissing the queen on the cheek. Ellen expressed her appreciation for the idea. "But there's one more thing we need to do," the king continued. "The guardians need to know the difference between a biography and an autobiography. That way they'll know that they don't have all the information about me."

The children thought this was a great idea. They worked with the king to send out a mission called Autobiographies.

What does *dispirited* mean?

What does it mean to tell a story in chronological order?

What's the trick for remembering the difference between an autobiography and a biography?

Chapter 6

Ellen found her mother in her study. She planned to ask the queen if she would like to help make a special dessert. Ellen had already asked Cook to supervise. Neither she nor her mother had had much practice baking.

When the queen saw her, she gushed, "Ellen! I'm so excited. I've decided to write a novel. You know how much I love mysteries. They could make a TV show based on the book. I could play the detective. Wouldn't that be grand?"

"Yes! So, have you started writing?"

The queen pointed at the screen on her desk. "Definitely!"

Ellen leaned in and read, "Chapter One."

When she looked confused, the queen explained. "I have a lot of notes. You remember your father making notes for his autobiography. Before you write the story, you have to outline. It's all sketched out."

"That's great!"

"I know. I'm hoping to write 3,000 words today."

"Wow, that seems like a lot. I was going to ask if you wanted to bake with me. It doesn't sound like you'll have time."

"I would love to bake with you. But would you be terribly disappointed if we baked another day?"

"Not at all. Cook said she would help."

"Thank you so much, Ellen." The queen hugged her daughter. When Ellen left, the queen started typing. She preferred typing over dictating.

That evening at dinner, Ellen and the queen were both excited. Ellen couldn't wait for the cake she had baked to be served.

"What is the name of the delicious dessert you've **devised**, Ellen?" the queen asked.

"It's Cook's **Consummate** Carrot Cake," Ellen said proudly.

"Carrot?" Luke asked, wondering how carrots in a cake could be consummate, whatever that meant.

"Yes! I shredded them myself, Luke."

When Luke looked even less excited about the cake, Ellen ignored him.

"Ellen, I'm sure it will be **delectable** and divine," the queen reassured her.

Ellen agreed it would be because it was Cook's special recipe. "How did the writing go, Mother? Did you finish 3,000 words?"

"As a matter of fact, I did." The queen beamed.

"What's this?" the king asked. "You've been writing? You didn't tell me."

The queen explained to the whole family that she had been working on a mystery book for some time. She said she had mostly been taking notes. She had wanted to wait until she had something written to tell them about it. Now she had a good start.

When everyone asked to hear what she had so far, she promised to read after they enjoyed dessert.

A carrot made of icing topped the cake, making Luke even more unsure about eating it. But when he took a bite, he was amazed. "Delish!" he praised it. Ellen was thrilled that everyone thought the carrot cake was wonderful. Of course, Cook listened by the door to the dining room to make sure it was well received. The king requested a second piece, ignoring his wife's raised eyebrows.

When he was finished, the queen used her tablet to share the beginning of her new mystery book.

"The name of the book is *Murder on the Galaxy Express*." Everyone oohed and aahed appreciatively. The queen cleared her throat and began to read.

★ ★ ★ ★ ★ ★ ★ ★ ★ ★

devised – *created*

consummate – *supreme*

delectable – *delicious*

★ ★ ★ ★ ★ ★ ★ ★ ★ ★

CHAPTER ONE

The calm, capable captain stood by the stern servant who was sending him to space. The captain, called Calhoun, was a huge, handsome man with hunky hair. All had heard of his heroic handiwork. But the servant, Steve, wasn't happy about helping this hero.

The moody man did not meddle with the confident captain, however. He lifted the last luggage into the loading loft. As Calhoun climbed the companionway, he called, "Communicate with the company for me." Under his breath, he called him a cad.

Calhoun concentrated on the cruise ahead. He settled into a seat next to a serious man whose name he learned was Stan. He also met a woman named Sally who stared suspiciously at him.

"That's all I have finished editing. I'm hugely happy it's happening, however," the queen said.

"I'm waiting and wondering about why Sally is staring suspiciously at him," Ellen said.

The king looked afraid to say anything but started with, "I'm very impressed, dear."

The queen didn't miss the concern in his voice. "You don't like it!" she said, disappointed.

"Not so! I think it's an impressive start."

"You already said that." The queen appeared hurt and made an excuse to leave the table.

"Uh-oh," Luke said. Even he knew that his father hadn't said the right thing about his mother's new book. "Don't you like it, Father? You can tell us." The other children nodded that their father could tell them the truth.

"It isn't at all that I don't like it. It's just that something seems wrong."

When the children asked him what he meant, he asked them if they had noticed anything strange about the book.

"Something sounds strange?" Luke asked.

"Yes. And it's not just the book. We seem to be sounding funny, too." The king had an idea and asked the children to hand him their mother's tablet. He silently read the passage again and nodded. "That explains it." He called for the guidebook to be brought to the dining room and then handed the tablet to Kirk. "Kirk, do you notice anything about the words in your mother's book?"

"Hm," he said looking them over. He was about to say no when he noticed that many words began with the same letter.

The king smiled when he mentioned this. Your mother is using a literary tool called alliteration. He read the children the entry on it when the guidebook was handed to him.

Alliteration
Alliteration is the use of the same consonant sound at the beginning of words that are close together. This literary device is found in writing and speaking. It is used to grab attention, create emotion, or persuade. Alliteration should not be overused unless children are the intended audience.
Alliteration is also used in tongue-twisters. These are sayings which are difficult to say—especially quickly.

"Oh. Mother's book isn't for children, is it?" Ellen asked.

"No," the king said, looking embarrassed for her. "I'll have to tell her what the problem is."

"It's surely a sad situation," Luke said. "Sorry to say so."

"Did you hear what you said, Luke?" Kirk asked. "You overused alliteration, too. Father, I need Screen to search stories swiftly. Ugh! Now I'm doing it."

Screen didn't find any news reports that would explain the excess alliteration. The king asked for live video from planet Sentence. In Noun Town, everything seemed to be in order. But Kirk spotted an unusual sign. He asked Screen to zoom in. Then they saw a street sign that read, "In Alphabetical Order, Under Penalty of Law."

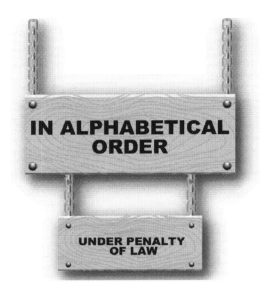

"What does 'under penalty of law' mean, Father?"

"It means they'll put the words in jail or fine them."

Luke felt bad for the words. He understood why they had put themselves in alphabetical order.

No one was surprised to see the same sign posted in Adjective Alley and Verb Village. "That explains it!" the king said. "Words that start with the same letter are together, causing excess alliteration. Your mother will be so relieved."

"But we have work to do. We have to get the guardians to help us with an alliteration mission. Otherwise, we'll all be selling seashells by the seashore," Kirk said. Everyone laughed.

What does *delectable* mean?

What's a tongue twister?

What are some sentences in this story that show alliteration?

32

Chapter 7

The queen couldn't remember her husband being so concerned about his appearance. He'd had a new suit custom-made for the premier of the new Star Battle movie. "You don't think it's too much, do you?" he asked, fidgeting with the sleeves.

"No, no, not at all," the queen answered sincerely. "You look so handsome. But you seem nervous."

"I guess I am. I've never been in a movie before." The producer of the sequel had contacted him two years before about making a **cameo** appearance in the film. The king hadn't hesitated to say yes.

★ ★ ★ ★ ★ ★ ★ ★ ★ ★

cameo – *brief*

★ ★ ★ ★ ★ ★ ★ ★ ★ ★

The three children had begged to go with him to the set, but the king had had to **decline**. He did **regale** them with stories of meeting the film's stars and working with a director. Luke especially complained that it was taking an eternity for the movie to be released. The king had to agree.

★ ★ ★ ★ ★ ★ ★ ★ ★ ★

decline – *say no*
regale – *entertain*

★ ★ ★ ★ ★ ★ ★ ★ ★ ★

But the premiere night had arrived. The press would be there and so would all the film's stars. This time the children would join him.

The king stepped onto the red carpet outside the Grammarwood Theater. Reporters peppered him with questions. "What was it like having to take orders from the director?" and "Do any of your children want to be actors?"

The king waved them off with a smile and ushered his family into the theater. Ellen and the queen politely discussed the beautiful gowns the women were wearing. The boys couldn't keep from pointing when they recognized a movie star. The king was so nervous that he didn't notice their bad manners.

Even though the king had a very small role, he and the royal family were seated in the front row. By the time the lights were dimmed, the king thought he might faint from the stress of it all. *What if the critics say I'm terrible?* he worried. But as the film's musical score filled the theater, he started to relax. He realized that he had no idea what the plot of the whole movie was. He only knew his small role. He decided to enjoy himself as he leaned back in his chair.

On the screen appeared the words: "This film has been rated family-friendly by the Galactic Rating Association."

The queen leaned over and whispered into the king's ear. "I'm so glad it's family-friendly. I completely forgot to check the ratings before we brought the children."

The king patted the queen's arm without turning his attention from the screen. He was thankful it was family-friendly, too.

When the stars of the original Star Battle movie appeared on screen, the theater erupted in applause. Ellen let out an extra-loud whistle, much to the embarrassment of the queen.

The hero of the movie and his friends were in the cockpit of a spaceship that was flying through space. Luke could hardly contain

34

himself. *When would the battle start?* he wondered. *When was his father's part? Did he get to fire at the enemy? That would be so cool!*

The hero pointed out the planets they passed. He talked about past battles they had fought together. The hero's friends agreed that those had been frightening times.

After twenty minutes of viewing space travel on the screen, the audience in the theater grew restless. Everyone was thrilled when the hero was contacted by the king of Grammar Galaxy. Ellen held back a scream of delight. That was her father in a *Star Battle* movie!

On screen, the king told the hero, "I just want you to know that you have my support. And you have the full support of the Galactic Forces."

The hero seemed thrilled to hear from the king. "Your Majesty, we thank you. We will let you know if we need your help. It's an honor to serve you. Truly."

The king was blushing in the darkness of the theater, but he thought he looked and sounded great. Light applause from the audience encouraged him further. Ellen and the queen hugged him. They were so proud.

Luke, however, was disappointed. *That was it?* Then he decided he was being silly to expect that his father would get to fly the spaceship or fire at an enemy. That was for the stars. He decided to focus on enjoying the rest of the movie, since his father's part was over.

"Are you hungry?" the movie hero asked his friends.

"Yeah, starving," they agreed.

The hero put the ship on autopilot and everyone left the cockpit to get something to eat. The audience was left staring at an empty cockpit.

Luke noticed that Kirk looked as bored as he felt. His father, though, was still smiling and seemed to be enjoying the movie. His mother shushed Luke when he asked if he could get some popcorn. He just had to wait for the characters to finish eating and come back to the cockpit.

When they did, he hoped to see some kind of explosion. Maybe an enemy had all their minds under his control. Maybe their ship would fail. But as Luke continued to watch, nothing changed. His eyes kept closing even as he tried to stay awake.

Sometime later, Kirk was shaking him. The lights were on in the theater. *Star Battle II* was over. "What did I miss?" Luke asked.

Kirk told him they would talk about it at home. Luke hoped they weren't mad at him for falling asleep during the best part of the movie.

When they arrived home, the queen asked Cook to prepare a snack for them. "I thought you were wonderful!" the queen said, hugging her husband again.

"Yes, you were great!" Ellen agreed.

"I'm so sorry I fell asleep, Father. Will you forgive me? Will you tell me what I missed?" Luke asked.

The king looked so unhappy that Luke wasn't sure he would forgive him. "You didn't miss anything, Luke," the king sighed.

"I didn't?"

"No. I have to admit that it was a terrible movie."

The queen was obviously relieved. "I'm so glad you thought so, too! I thought maybe it just wasn't my type of movie. I didn't see the first one."

"No, it was terrible," the king said again.

"It was nothing like the first one," Kirk said. "But sequels are often bad, right, Father?"

"Yes, but this was more than just it being a sequel."

"You don't think it was because you were in it, do you?" Luke asked.

"At first I did. But the more I thought about it, I realized that something else is really wrong with this movie."

"Remember when the Gremlin mixed up the characters, settings, and plots of books? Is that what's wrong?" Kirk asked.

"That can't be it," Luke answered. "The characters of *Star Battle* were the same. So was the setting."

"But what about the plot? Something was definitely wrong with the plot," Kirk said.

"What's a plot again?" Luke asked.

Kirk reminded him that the plot of a story is the problem and the solution.

"That's right, Luke," the king said. "But there is more you need to know about plots." He asked for the guidebook to be brought to the dining room. When it arrived, he read the entry for story action.

Story Action

Exposition is the information presented at the beginning of a story. It explains past events and helps readers or viewers understand the rest of the story. You can remember what exposition is by thinking of an expo which is a show. Exposition shows important information.

Rising action begins immediately after the exposition. It starts the plot and includes everything that creates interest and suspense.

Climax is a Greek word meaning ladder. A climax is when the rising action has the most conflict or suspense.

Falling action is what happens after the climax.

The resolution is how the story ends.

"I saw some exposition in *Star Battle II*," Luke said. "Like when the characters came onto the screen. They talked about past battles."

"That's right, Luke," the king answered.

"I didn't see any rising action, though," Kirk added, shaking his head.

"Yeah, and what was the climax?" Ellen asked. "Was it when you were on, Father?"

The king laughed. "It was for me, but I don't think it was supposed to be. There was no rising action or climax in this movie. That's why it was so bad. The question is why? Why didn't anything exciting happen in a *Star Battle* movie?"

"Dear, was the first *Star Battle* movie family-friendly?" the queen asked.

The king didn't know, so he asked Screen to look it up. When he learned that it wasn't, he shook his head. "The director must have thought that family-friendly meant no action! That's not what it means. This movie will be a box-office bomb."

"A bomb is too exciting a term for this movie," Kirk said. He apologized when his father looked upset. "Is there anything we can do, Father?"

"There just might be. If you can get the guardians to convince the director to reshoot the movie, we might be able to rescue it. You'll need to send out a mission on story action right away."

The children agreed and got to work, hoping that a new, improved Star Battle movie would be in theaters soon.

What does *decline* mean in the story?

What was wrong with the *Star Battle* movie?

Why did the king think the director left all the action out of the movie?

Chapter 8

Kirk was delighted when he received an envelope in the mail addressed to him. Most **correspondence** was electronic. He **surmised** that this was something important because the envelope had elegant lettering.

He didn't know what to think when he read the letter inside.

★ ★ ★ ★ ★ ★ ★ ★ ★ ★ ★
correspondence – *mail*
surmised – *guessed*
★ ★ ★ ★ ★ ★ ★ ★ ★ ★ ★

Theater Royal Company

Dear Kirk English,

I am writing today to invite you to play the role of Romeo in our upcoming production of Romeo and Juliet. We would be so honored if you would accept the role. We would like to begin rehearsals soon. Please contact me with any questions you have at your earliest convenience.

Regards,
Director of the Royal Theater Company

Kirk didn't know whether to be thrilled or depressed. He had never been in a play. Why would the Theater Company want *him*? Maybe they were really hoping he would say no. He decided to ask his parents about it at dinner that evening.

After Kirk read his family the letter, his mother applauded in delight. His father beamed, obviously proud of his son.

"So you think I should say yes?" Kirk asked.

"Of course!" his parents answered in unison.

"This is such an honor," the queen gushed.

"Indeed!" the king agreed.

"You don't think it's a problem that I've never been in a play before?" Kirk asked.

"They wouldn't have invited you if they didn't think you were perfect for the role," the king said.

The queen agreed. "Yes, I think you'll be an amazing Romeo, Kirk. Romeo is handsome and smart just like you. Wait until I tell my friends!" Kirk blushed.

Kirk accepted the role but grew more and more **apprehensive** about the play. He wished he could tell the director he'd changed his mind, but he didn't want to disappoint his parents.

★ ★ ★ ★ ★ ★ ★ ★ ★ ★
apprehensive – *nervous*
★ ★ ★ ★ ★ ★ ★ ★ ★ ★

The first rehearsal day arrived and Kirk decided to make the best of it. The director asked each participant to introduce themselves and their role. Kirk was glad his parents had taught him how to introduce himself. He did fine with that but was embarrassed to admit that he would be playing Romeo.

Everyone was very nice, however. Kirk was given some paperwork and was then measured for his costume. He was relieved that the first meeting was over and that he had survived. He hoped the next meetings would go as well.

The next rehearsal was just for Kirk and the girl playing Juliet. That was a relief for Kirk. If he was going to make mistakes at first, at least it wouldn't be in front of the whole group.

"Okay, Romeo and Juliet. Let's run through your lines at the end of Scene Five, Act I, right after Tybalt exits," the director said.

The girl playing Juliet climbed the steps to the stage, so Kirk joined her.

"Where's your script?" the director asked.

Kirk felt sick. *What is a script?* he wondered.

"Did you forget it? No problem. Use this one," the director said, handing him a binder.

This must be a script, Kirk thought.

"Read your part," the director urged him.

Kirk scanned the page in front of him until he saw some sentences listed after ROMEO. He read uncertainly. "If I profane with my unworthiest hand this holy shrine, the gentle fine is this: My lips, two blushing pilgrims, ready stand to smooth that rough touch with a tender kiss."

When he looked confused, the director said, "Kirk, it's Shakespeare. It's normal if you don't understand it." Kirk smiled with relief. "Okay, before we continue, I'm going to have you both move stage right." Kirk started walking to the director's right. "Uh, Kirk, stage right is your right when you're facing the audience."

"Oh, of course," Kirk said, embarrassed again.

"Okay, now if you'd both come down stage." Kirk quickly jumped down from the stage. The director tried not to laugh. "Kirk, down stage means staying on stage, but closer to the audience."

"Oh, I'm sorry," Kirk said, getting back on stage.

"Hey, not a problem, Kirk. We're just thrilled to have you as part of the cast."

Kirk wondered if someone in the play had a broken bone. Was everyone going to be signing that person's cast?

"Let's run some more lines," the director said. Kirk looked at the floor but didn't see any lines he could run. Very slowly the director said, "Read your part from the script."

"Oh, yes! Of course." Kirk read more of the sentences listed after ROMEO in the script that he didn't understand.

Finally, the director said they were finished for the night. He encouraged the two to begin memorizing their parts.

Kirk was exhausted when he got home. His family was eager to hear what he thought. He kept saying it had been fine until he finally exploded. "It was terrible! I didn't even know it was a script. What's stage right? What's down stage? I didn't know. I looked so foolish. I thought running lines was running on lines!" His family looked sorry for him. "What's even worse is I have no idea what I'm saying. 'That's Shakespeare,' the director said. I don't get it!"

The king put his arm around Kirk. "Son, I apologize. I didn't prepare you for this. Shakespeare's play uses 16th century English. The language has changed since then, but Romeo and Juliet is also a play that sounds like poetry."

"That's not the part that upset me the most. It was not knowing what the director was saying."

"I see," the king said. "I have a feeling you aren't the only one who doesn't know drama terms." The king requested the guidebook be brought to them. He read the "Drama Terms" entry.

Drama Terms
A **drama** is a story acted out on a stage or for film. A **cast** is the group of actors and actresses who play the characters in the story.
An **act** is a main part of a play that includes several scenes. **Scenes** happen in one place or time. The **set** (background and objects on stage) may change for different scenes. **Props** are objects characters use on stage.
Scripts for plays include lines (what the characters say). They also include **stage directions** (what the characters do). A **narrator** tells what's happening in the story.
A **curtain call** happens at the end of the play. The actors all appear on stage to be applauded by the audience.

"That helps a lot. I can imagine not knowing what a prop is. Now I won't look so foolish," Kirk said.

"I can't wait for you to have a curtain call!" Ellen exclaimed. Kirk smiled appreciatively.

"Father? Do you think it's important to know these terms even if you're not playing Romeo?" Kirk asked.

"I certainly do," the king said.

The three children sent out a mission they called Drama Terms.

What does *surmised* mean?

Why was Kirk most upset about being in the play?

Would you like to be an actor or actress in a play?

Unit II: Adventures in Spelling Vocabulary

Chapter 9

The children were excited that they would be taking the royal carriage around their city for the day. Their father said it was a beautiful day and it would be good for the citizens of the planet to see them. They were also excited that Comet could join them.

They passed by the main library branch first. A few children outside the library noticed them and ran toward them, waving. The queen said they should have brought candy for the children. But the king **vehemently**

★ ★ ★ ★ ★ ★ ★ ★ ★ ★
vehemently – *strongly*
★ ★ ★ ★ ★ ★ ★ ★ ★ ★

disagreed. Children had too much candy already, he said.

The driver asked the king where he wanted to go next. He told him to make the big loop. The city's main attractions were laid out in a large circle. The first area they came to was the Old City. The historical buildings were the children's favorite. It was also where the ice cream shop was located. They usually made a stop there on their way home. Luke had to keep himself from asking if they could stop immediately.

As the carriage slowly made its way down the stone streets, the Old City came into view. There were small shops and boutiques with goods displayed in the windows. Ellen and the queen exclaimed over the beautiful dresses on the mannequins. Luke drooled as they passed an old-fashioned candy shop. Its homemade fudge was just as tempting as the ice cream.

Next, they came to the old barber shop. The king erupted in a fit of laughter. He held his stomach and **guffawed**, unable to answer his family's questions about what was so funny. But he pointed at the sign in the barber shop as they slowly passed by.

★ ★ ★ ★ ★ ★ ★ ★ ★ ★

guffawed – *laughed*

stifled – *silenced*

★ ★ ★ ★ ★ ★ ★ ★ ★ ★

"Hare cuts $10," Luke read out loud. "Why is that funny?"

When the king caught his breath, he explained that it was misspelled. Luke didn't think anything to do with spelling was funny. He found it difficult to spell. The king noticed Luke's frown. He said, "I shouldn't laugh when people make spelling errors."

Luke seemed less upset and the king was glad. He hoped to make this a great outing for the family, so he **stifled** continued laughter.

The family continued through the Old City. The queen pointed out the brightly colored, fresh flowers on the street. She was going to suggest they stop to buy some when she noticed the sign above the store. It read: Flour Shop. "Flour shop?" she said out loud. Then she began to giggle. She patted the king's arm and pointed at the sign. He joined her in laughing to the point that they were both nearly in tears.

"What is going on?" Luke asked. He was irritated until he thought a moment. "Father, I think I know what's going on! The Gremlin must have released laughing gas in the Old City because he knew we were coming. We have to leave immediately!"

The king tried to be serious. "Luke, we are laughing at another spelling mistake. I'm sorry. It can't be laughing gas because you aren't laughing."

Luke was relieved and annoyed. He was glad there was no laughing gas. But it bothered him that his father thought misspelled words were so funny. He was able to forget about it when his father suggested they stop and go into the old bookstore.

The whole family enjoyed browsing the shelves. They got most of their books from the library but loved buying books, too. Each of them went looking for the types of books they loved most. The king found the biography section. The queen was looking at mysteries. Kirk hoped to find a new robotics book. Ellen wanted to find some Nancy Drew books. Her mother had said they were mystery books she would enjoy. Luke was interested in finding some funny fiction.

After they each found a book they were interested in purchasing, they met near the checkout. Ellen noticed a display of notebooks. "Oh, Mother, I need a new notebook. May I buy one?" she pleaded. When her mother agreed, she chose one with a floral cover. The queen took it and giggled. When she showed it to her husband, he started laughing with her.

It was Ellen's turn to be annoyed. "What's so funny?" she asked her parents.

"It says 'Deer Diary,'" the queen said in between giggles.

When Ellen remained confused, the queen explained that the title was misspelled. Ellen didn't see the humor in it and put the notebook back. The queen was sorry she had offended her daughter.

When the family got back into the carriage, the queen told her husband that they had to stop making fun of spelling errors. He agreed. They had a lovely time riding around the rest of the day. They saw the theater, the stadium, and the entrances to the zoo and the gardens. The children's hard feelings were completely forgotten when they stopped for ice cream.

That evening the queen gathered everyone in the media room. She'd learned the news planned a story on the royal family's ride around the city. The children were excited when they saw themselves on TV. The camera zoomed in on Kirk as he was walking into the bookstore. Underneath his image was the caption, "Air Apparent." The announcer talked about Kirk spending his time in the robotics section of the bookstore. The footage switched to the family enjoying ice cream together.

"I really don't like them showing me eating," the queen said, frowning.

"I really don't like them calling Kirk an air," the king said, laughing.

Kirk was shocked. "I am an heir, though."

"Yes, of course, you are! But they misspelled it," the king explained.

Kirk wondered to himself if his parents were being overly concerned about spelling errors.

The newscast had shifted to a different story. "SoundSpell is a new app that is getting millions of downloads a month," the reporter said. "Rather than entering letters to find a word's spelling, you say the word. The app gives you the spelling automatically."

"Cool!" Luke exclaimed. "I need that app!"

A young boy demonstrated the app by saying the word *peace*. He showed the word's spelling to the camera. "And look," he said. "It will say the spelling for you, too."

"So that's what's going on," the king said. "You were right, Luke. This misspelling business isn't funny. I suspect the Gremlin is behind the SoundSpell app."

"Why would the Gremlin want kids to be able to spell?" Luke asked.

"He doesn't. He wants them to misspell homophones." After the guidebook was brought to him, he read the entry on homophones to the children.

Homophones
Homo is Greek for same and *phon* is Greek for sound. Homophones are words that sound the same. But they have different meanings, spellings, or both. Homophones are homonyms, which is Greek for same name or word. Some frequently confused homophones are: to, two, too there, their, they're your, you're

> its, it's
> **See also:** Homographs

The king pointed out the different spellings of the homophones. "T-o is used for going to. T-w-o is a number. T-o-o means also or overly. I remember that t-o-o means also by thinking that the second *o* wants to go along with the first. It wants to go, too."

The children said that that was a good way to remember how to spell it. The king continued, "Notice how there, t-h-e-r-e has the word *here* in it. So *there* means a place. T-h-e-i-r has the word *heir* in it. That's what the newscast misspelled, Kirk. They used the homophone a-i-r which means what we breathe. The word *heir* means that the throne belongs to him next. That helps me to remember that t-h-e-i-r means belonging to them."

"Father, doesn't h-e-i-r also mean that the throne belongs to her next?" Ellen asked.

"Indeed!" the king replied. Ellen made sure her brothers heard this. "Now then, t-h-e-y apostrophe r-e stands for they are. Remember the apostrophe stands for *a* in this contraction." When the children nodded, he continued. "Y-o-u-r means belongs to you. Y-o-u apostrophe r-e—"

"Means you are!" Luke interrupted.

"Right you are, Luke," the king answered. "I-t-s means belonging to it. And what does i-t apostrophe *s* mean, Luke?"

"It is. It says 'see also homographs.' I remember what those are. They're words that are spelled the same. But they might be said differently or have different meanings. Right, Father?" Luke said.

"Correct!" the king said approvingly.

"So the SoundSpell app is causing people to misspell homophones. And the result is they aren't writing what they mean?" Kirk asked.

"Yes, Kirk, I'm afraid so."

"What do we do about it?" Kirk asked. Before the king could respond, he answered his own question. "I know we have to get the guardians involved," he said, smiling. "But what about the app?"

"I don't know that I can legally shut it down. But perhaps we could get the guardians to force the developers to improve it," the king explained.

The king helped the children create a mission called Homophones. He said he knew he should be eager to stop the misspellings. But he admitted that he was a little sad about it, too. The SoundSpell app had made him laugh more than he had in years.

What does *guffawed* mean?

What was funny about the sign that said, "Hare Cuts $10"? What was funny about the notebook title, *Deer Diary*?

How can you remember how the word *too* is spelled?

Chapter 10

Kirk rushed into the sunroom where his parents were reading, so he could show them his work. He put a robot down on the floor and commanded it to spin. It did. Comet immediately started barking.

"Wow, Kirk, did you program it to do that?" the king asked.

"I did!" Kirk said with pride.

"That's wonderful, dear," the queen told him. "We're very proud of you."

"T-Y," Kirk said.

"T-Y?" the queen said.

Just then Kirk's communicator buzzed. He looked at it and saw that it was his friend. "Oh, I have to show Jim what it can do. B-R-B." Kirk scooped up the robot and left the room.

"B-R-B?" the queen repeated. "What is he saying, dear?"

"Oh, it's that new teen talk," the king answered.

The queen nodded like she understood, but she looked worried.

A few minutes later Cook rushed into the room, **hysterical**. She kept talking about Ellen. The queen calmed her down enough to get her to explain what happened. "Ellen—she came to the

★ ★ ★ ★ ★ ★ ★ ★ ★ ★

hysterical – *panicky*

★ ★ ★ ★ ★ ★ ★ ★ ★ ★

kitchen. She asked for a BLT. Oh, I should have made her one!" she wailed. When the queen hugged her and said it was all right, she continued. "So I said, how about a PBJ instead? You can make it yourself. I'm so sorry! I shouldn't have let her climb up to get the peanut butter!"

"Did she fall?" the queen said. She tried not to be too alarmed for Cook's sake.

"Yes, yes, she fell. And the MD is MIA!" Cook explained that Ellen was in the castle **infirmary**, and the nurse said she needed a doctor ASAP.

★ ★ ★ ★ ★ ★ ★ ★ ★ ★

infirmary – *hospital*
fracture – *break*

★ ★ ★ ★ ★ ★ ★ ★ ★ ★

The king and queen got to Ellen quickly and found her with an ice pack on her lower back. The nurse explained that she had landed on her tailbone. She wanted Ellen to have an x-ray. She had already called ahead to the nearest urgent care center for them. The king asked the nurse to make sure the boys knew where they were going. The three took the spacecopter and arrived at the clinic quickly.

Once in the waiting area, the receptionist said she had been expecting them. She handed the queen some paperwork. "I'll need her DOB, the name of her MD, her meds and OTCs, and a CC for payment."

The queen hadn't completed paperwork in a very long time. She honestly didn't know what the receptionist was saying. She looked to her husband for help.

"We are the royal family. Can't we skip the paperwork and just get the x-ray?" the king asked.

"SOP," the receptionist said apologetically.

"SOP?" the king repeated. He gave up and began completing the forms while they waited for Ellen to be seen.

After her x-ray was done, the doctor called them back to talk to them. "Good news!" she said. "She hit her tailbone pretty hard. She will be sore, but there is no **fracture**." The three expressed relief at the news. "So all she needs is some R&R and TLC. You can give her something OTC for pain if she needs it, too." The queen nodded like she knew what she was talking about. The doctor handed her a brochure. "FYI here are some answers to some FAQs. Of course, you can always call us." The doctor shook hands with the king and queen. She patted Ellen on the shoulder and left the room.

The three of them returned home. The queen said she really missed their physician and hoped he returned quickly. "I didn't understand any of that medical talk."

After the queen helped Ellen get comfortable in the media room, Cook arrived with a BLT for her. "I'm so sorry, Ellen!" she said, crying.

Ellen was able to reassure her that the fall hadn't been her fault at all. "I love PBJs, too. But I am hungry. Thank you, Cook." Ellen hugged her and Cook smiled.

"Would you like some OJ, too?" When Ellen agreed, Cook left to get it for her.

The boys passed her coming into the room. "Are you okay, El?" Luke asked. Ellen nodded but was glad her brother was concerned.

Kirk asked her about the pain. "When do they think you'll feel better?"

"That's T-B-D," Ellen answered.

"Is that teen talk, too?" the queen asked, feeling annoyed. "All day people have been saying things I don't understand. B-R-B, O-T-C, and now T-B-D."

The king reassured her. "Some of it is teen talk, dear. But you are right that people have been using a lot of acronyms today. Kirk, I think we need to investigate."

They asked Screen to search for news events from across the galaxy. Nothing appeared unusual. But Ellen begged them to show the circus that was performing on planet Spelling.

Soon a live feed of a man and woman on a high wire appeared. They slowly walked toward one another. When they met in the middle, they held up the letters Y and W.

"What in the galaxy does that mean?" the queen asked.

"You're welcome," Kirk and Ellen said in unison.

"For what? You didn't tell me what it means," the queen said, continuing to sound irritated.

"You've had a long day, dear," the king said. "Would you like to relax and read for a while?"

The queen sighed. "Yes, I would, dear. Thank you."

"Y-W," the king said.

The queen looked hurt as she left the room.

"Well, now I know this circus is causing problems," the king said. When the children asked why he explained. "I didn't intend to say Y-W and upset your mother. It just came out."

"That happens to me all the time," Luke said. His three family members laughed.

"How is the circus causing problems, Father?" Ellen asked.

"These acrobats appear to be using letters in their act," the king said, pointing to the screen. Three women were performing on rings in the air. They each held a letter between their feet. It read, "TBA."

"What does that mean?" Ellen asked.

"To be announced," the king answered.

"Okay. When will you tell us?" Ellen asked.

The king responded by having the guidebook brought to him. He read the entry called "Acronyms."

Acronyms

Acro is Greek for highest point, top, or outermost. Nym is Greek for name or word. Acronyms are words made up of the first letter of words in a phrase. Acronyms are a form of abbreviation or shortened form of a word. Using them can lead to confusion if they aren't widely recognized.

Many state abbreviations are acronyms, like NY for New York. Some countries are also abbreviated with an acronym, such as USA for United States of America.

New acronyms have developed as a result of text messaging. Some common texting acronyms include:

TY – thank you	BRB – be right back	YW – you're welcome
LOL – laughing out loud	NP – no problem	WTG – way to go

Some other common acronyms are listed below:

BLT – bacon, lettuce, tomato sandwich	PBJ – peanut butter and jelly sandwich
DOB – date of birth	MD – medical doctor
MIA – missing in action	OTC – over the counter
CC – credit card	SOP – standard operating procedure
FYI – for your information	FAQ – frequently asked questions
ASAP – as soon as possible	R&R – rest and relaxation
TLC – tender loving care	TBD – to be determined
OJ – orange juice	SOS – save our souls

"Acronyms can save time. That's a good thing, right?" Ellen asked.

"Yes, but they are confusing when you use them with people who don't know them," Kirk added.

"It's almost like speaking a foreign language," Luke suggested.

"Yes. I don't like the overuse of them that is occurring because of the circus. I'm going to see what I can do about that. But the guardians have work to do," the king said.

"We're sending out an SOS!" Ellen exclaimed. The three of them began working on an acronyms mission to be sent out ASAP.

What does *hysterical* mean?

Which of the acronyms in the guidebook do you use the most?

Why was the queen upset?

Chapter II

The king was **absorbed** in a game of football. He was watching on the screen in the media room. The queen entered the room and asked, "What are you doing, dear?" He didn't answer, so she asked louder. When he still didn't answer, she got between him and the screen.

His answer was, "I'm watching football, of course." He appeared to be very interested in watching the rest of the game.

The queen's brow wrinkled in a mix of concern and annoyance. "You didn't hear me when I came in."

★ ★ ★ ★ ★ ★ ★ ★ ★ ★

absorbed – *interested*

★ ★ ★ ★ ★ ★ ★ ★ ★ ★

"I was watching the game."

"But even when I was much louder you didn't hear me," the queen insisted.

"Are you trying to say there's something wrong with my hearing?"

"Yes!" the queen replied, hands on hips.

"That's ridiculous," he answered, waving her away.

"You're not as young as you used to be."

The king sighed. "If you'll let me finish watching the game, I'll see a doctor."

"You will?" the queen was relieved. She kissed her husband on the cheek and left him to his game.

Once in her study, the queen asked Screen to research hearing specialists. The top result was a man listed as a geologist. That didn't seem right. But when she read about his **expertise**, testing and treating hearing disorders were listed. His patients gave him good reviews, too. She contacted the office and made an appointment for her husband. She decided not to mention it until the morning of the appointment. That way he wouldn't be tempted to change his mind.

★ ★ ★ ★ ★ ★ ★ ★ ★ ★

expertise – *skill*

★ ★ ★ ★ ★ ★ ★ ★ ★ ★

Just as she thought, he tried to get out of the appointment. "There is nothing wrong with my hearing!" he yelled.

"Why are you so loud then?" the queen asked.

"Because this is just a waste of my time and money."

"You promised you'd go."

The king sighed again. "You aren't going to give up on this until I go, are you?"

The queen smiled and shook her head.

The two took the spacecopter. The king said they could use the spaceporter, but they would waste time waiting anyway. On the way, the king told her that she'd see this appointment was unnecessary.

When the two of them arrived at the doctor's office, the king laughed. "He's a geologist. That's not an ear doctor." The queen insisted that he was listed as the best in the city. The king thought maybe someone was playing a practical joke on him. "Oh, okay. I'll see the geologist to have my ears tested." He winked at the queen, who just shrugged in response.

The king filled out the paperwork, which seemed to be in order. But at the end of the form was a line for his astrograph. He pointed it out to the queen. "Astrograph. Hilarious! Okay. I'll play along."

The paperwork was turned in for fifteen minutes. Then a woman came and asked them to come back to wait for the doctor.

"I'm sure he's a doctor," the king mumbled. "Where's the hidden camera?" When the doctor finally came in, the king was surprised that he did indeed seem to be an MD.

"Now what brings you in today, Your Majesties? I must say it's a **privilege** to serve the royal family."

★ ★ ★ ★ ★ ★ ★ ★ ★ ★

privilege –*honor*

★ ★ ★ ★ ★ ★ ★ ★ ★ ★

Before the king could dismiss him, she answered, "Yes, thank you. The king has had some signs of hearing loss. He doesn't think so."

"She's right. I don't. I'm sure you'll find that I'm normal."

"Your Majesty, it's common for those suffering hearing loss not to recognize it."

The king seemed a little embarrassed. To try to relax him, the doctor said, "I really did enjoy your videography."

"What?" the king asked, confused. The doctor looked knowingly at the queen. "What I'll do now is put an instrument in your ears that will take a philograph. That will help me determine if you have hearing loss."

"What? That makes no sense!" The king was getting more upset.

"Often people with hearing loss find things stop making sense," the doctor reassured him.

The king let the doctor examine his ears, hoping he could get the appointment over with faster. When he asked if the exam showed anything, the doctor said he wanted to do another test. "We'll inject a dye through a phone in your arm. Then we'll do a scan of your head."

"What? This is crazy! Dear, does this make sense to you?"

The queen patted her husband's arm. "I just want to help you hear as well as you used to."

The king gave up and agreed to the scan of his head. Afterward, the doctor told him he would call with the results in a few days.

When the royal couple returned home, the three children were there to greet them.

"Is your hearing okay, Father?" Ellen asked after hugging him.

"Of course it is!" he answered gruffly.

"We'll know in a couple of days," the queen said, putting her arm around Ellen.

"Something's wrong," the king said, thinking aloud.

"Now, dear, don't worry," the queen said. "Whatever is wrong with your hearing can be treated."

"That's not what I mean. The whole trip to the clinic wasn't a joke, right?" When the queen agreed, he continued. "They were using words all wrong. They didn't make sense. Geologists don't treat hearing disorders. They said they were going to put dye in my vein through a phone!"

"What do you think is happening, Father?" Kirk asked.

"I don't know yet, but I'm going to find out." He asked Screen for the definition of geologist and was given: "a doctor who tests hearing and treats disorders of the ears."

"That's wrong!" the king said, frustrated.

"Could the Gremlin have tampered with our dictionaries?' Kirk asked.

"Yes, but I have a feeling that it's not the dictionaries this time."

He asked Screen for the definition of a geophile and was told, "Someone who loves and is particular about music and sound."

"That explains it!" the king said, seeming very relieved.

"What is it?" Kirk asked.

"I will tell you as soon as I find the source of the problem. Screen, open the Word Ancestry site, please."

"You're looking up the history of words?" Ellen asked.

"No, I'm looking up word roots." The website displayed a graphic of a tree underneath the headline, "Find the roots of any word." The king asked Screen to search for the root *phon*. The words phonable, transphontation, phoner and others appeared in the tree. At the top of the tree was the notation, "Phon is Greek for carry."

"Aha!" the king cried. He asked for the guidebook to be brought to him so he could explain what he'd found. "Word Ancestry is our archive for information on root words. Here's what the guidebook tells us about them."

Root Words

A root word is the main word that prefixes and suffixes are added to. Learning meanings of Greek and Latin root words can build a student's vocabulary. Some common root words and their meanings are:

ast – star	audi – hear	auto – self
bio – life	dict – say	geo – earth
graph – write	phil – love	phon – sound
photo – light	port – carry	vid or vis – see
logo – word/study		

Learning the meanings of prefixes (added to the beginning of words) and suffixes (added to the end of words) also builds vocabulary.

"The Word Ancestry site has been tampered with. Root words have been switched. Now people are saying and writing what they don't mean," the king explained.

"If many root words have been changed, it could take forever to fix the website," Luke said.

"Not if the guardians help us," Ellen said.

"We're going to need to improve the website's security too, aren't we, Father?"

"Indeed! I'll contact our head programmer immediately."

The three children began working on a mission called Root Words.

A while later, Cook announced it was time for dinner. "I definitely heard that!" the king declared.

What does *privilege* mean?

Instead of a philograph, what was the doctor going to take of the inside of the king's ears?

Why didn't the king understand the doctor?

Chapter 12

It was a rainy Saturday morning and the king suggested they go to the art museum. He was very much an art **connoisseur** with his own castle gallery. It had been a while since they had been, so the rest of the family cheerfully agreed to go.

They used the spaceporter because of the weather. They soon appeared at the visitor entrance. When one of the **docents** recognized them, she greeted them warmly. She asked which areas of the museum they were most interested in seeing. When the king answered her, he was astonished to see her do a backbend.

"You're really flexible!" Luke exclaimed.

"Thank you," she said, standing up and smoothing her jacket. "Now let's go to the European art section that you're interested in."

The royal family walked through the exhibits. They heard explanations of the artwork as they went. The queen said, "Some of these paintings tell stories, don't they, dear."

The king agreed. "You know what they say. A picture paints a thousand words."

Words began covering the painting they were looking at. When the queen asked the king about it, he said that they must have gotten too close to it. It was a new security measure, he thought.

After an hour of looking at paintings and sculptures, the king looked at a clock on the wall. "Time sure flies when you're here, doesn't it?" The clock flew across the room, seeming to be suspended on a wire of some sort. Ellen and the queen were so startled that they screamed.

The king asked the docent about the clock. She said that it had never happened before. She appeared nervous and tried to distract the king by asking him what other exhibits he would like to see. He told her he would like to see the ancient art exhibits. She seemed pleased with his choice and led the family to that area of the museum.

The docent spent some time telling them about the museum's ancient art. Then Luke asked, "Which do you like better, Father— European or ancient art?"

"Oh, Luke," the king shrugged. "That's like comparing apples and oranges." Luke was surprised that his father had fruit in his hands to show him. He wasn't a big fruit eater.

"You must be hungry," Luke suggested.

The king couldn't stop staring at the fruit in his hands. "I didn't bring this, did I?" He told the docent, "I think it's a good time for a lunch break." He hoped to leave the fruit in the restaurant.

The docent responded by doing another backbend. When she stood up, she rushed ahead of the family to make arrangements for their meal.

When she had gone, the queen whispered, "She seems to do backbends at the drop of a hat." A hat fell on the floor at their feet. "Where did this come from?" she asked, looking around.

"I'm sure it blew in from a clothing exhibit nearby," the king said.

"There aren't any clothing exhibits here," she said.

The king encouraged her to come with him and eat. He had no explanation for the hat, but it didn't worry him.

The museum restaurant had a beautiful view of a fountain and the surrounding grounds.

"What a great place to hang out," Kirk said. He walked over to a small window on the right side, opened it, and stuck his head out.

"Kirk, what are you doing?" his mother chastised him. "Close that window!"

Kirk complied and looked embarrassed. Meanwhile, the docent was speaking to the chef about what they would serve to the royal family. "I want to serve something that will knock the queen's socks off." The chef agreed and started giving his kitchen staff **directives**.

★ ★ ★ ★ ★ ★ ★ ★ ★

directives – *orders*

★ ★ ★ ★ ★ ★ ★ ★ ★

The docent went to tell the family that lunch would be served shortly. She found the queen trying to put her stockings back on. "I don't understand how they came off," she was muttering. "They must have bad elastic."

"Uh, Father," Luke said, tapping the king on the shoulder. "Look outside." He was astonished to see hundreds of dogs and cats falling from the sky.

"It's raining cats and dogs," the queen said wonderingly. "Are you thinking what I'm thinking?" she asked the king.

"Unfortunately, yes. Children, we have to return to the castle immediately. There is something seriously wrong in the galaxy."

The king made his apologies to the docent and the five of them appeared back at the castle. The king led them to the castle library where he retrieved the guidebook. He looked up idioms and had Kirk read the entry.

Idioms

An idiom is an expression that means something other than its words indicate. For example, the saying *it costs an arm and a leg* means it's expensive, not that an arm and a leg are required for payment. Some other common idioms are listed below.

Back to the drawing board	**The ball is in your court**
Start over because your first attempt failed	*It's your turn to speak or act*
You're barking up the wrong tree	**Bit off more than you can chew**
You have the wrong person/place	*It's too much for you*
Can't judge a book by its cover	**Hit the nail on the head**
You can't tell everything by appearance	*Said/did something exactly right*
Cross that bridge when you come to it	**Feel under the weather**
Don't worry about what you'll do later	*Feel sick*
It's raining cats and dogs	**Bend over backward**
It's raining hard	*Do everything you can*
Comparing apples and oranges	**The drop of a hat**
Comparing two different things	*All the time*
Hanging out	**Picture paints a thousand words**
Spending time with	*Picture gives a lot of information*
Time flies	**Piece of cake**
Time seems to go quickly	*Easy*
Don't count your chickens before they've hatched	
Don't plan for something that may not happen	

"Idioms are literally happening, right, Father? But why?" Ellen asked.

"I don't know. Screen, give me anything you have on idioms." A dictionary entry for idioms appeared on the screen. It read, "An offensive phrase that is no longer used in Grammar Galaxy."

"What?!" the king exclaimed. "How could they think idiom is an offensive word?"

"Could they have it confused with the word idiot?" Kirk asked.

"Maybe. But how could they get them confused? Unless the Gremlin is behind this." The king sighed. "Screen, show me Idiom Isle on planet Sentence." While the king waited, he explained. "Idioms live on their own island where they can't confuse anyone. Everyone knows not to take them seriously."

Screen showed video footage of idioms being ferried off the island. A reporter stood near the dock, describing the scene. Men and women carried signs that read, "They're not idioms; they're words" and "Words deserve freedom."

"They're letting the idioms off the island," Kirk said.

"But why do they have to stay on the island, Father? I wouldn't want to stay on an island forever," Ellen said.

"Ellen, Idiom Isle is paradise. These words aren't being mistreated. But now we have a crisis. We won't be able to tell the difference between idioms and other words."

"Can't the guardians help?" Luke asked.

The king smiled and put his arm around Luke. "Yes, they can. Will you create a mission for them? I'll send Grammar Patrol to planet Sentence to escort the idioms back to the island. They'll need a list of idioms from the guardians."

When the three children got to work, the king announced he was going to get some lunch. "I'm so hungry I could eat a —."

"Don't!" they yelled. The king was grateful for the warning.

What does *connoisseur* mean?

Why did Kirk hang his head out the window?

What was the king going to say: "I'm so hungry I could eat a —"?

Chapter 13

It was a chilly morning when Kirk was late coming to breakfast. The other children had already been excused. He apologized and explained, "My computer wasn't working and I couldn't figure it out. I finally cleared the cashay and got it working."

"The what?" the queen asked before reminding Kirk to put his napkin on his lap.

"The cashay. It's temporary computer memory."

"I have no idea what you're talking about."

Kirk laughed. "It's computer stuff, Mother."

The king was reading the paper and not paying attention. The queen had told him many times before that it bothered her when he read at the table. She sighed loudly to indicate her displeasure, but the king didn't flinch.

Meanwhile, Cook brought Kirk an after-breakfast menu. The Queen told Cook that they could bring him anything at all since he was late, but Cook said it was no trouble. Kirk looked over the menu and asked Cook to bring him rasp-berry muffins and hot coco-uh.

The queen stifled a laugh. When Kirk asked what was so funny, the queen explained. "You mispronounced words. We don't make the *p* sound in raspberry or the short *u* sound for the *a* in cocoa."

When Kirk seemed offended, she apologized for laughing. She decided to spend time talking with her son while he ate. It wasn't often that she could focus solely on her eldest son. "What have you been reading lately, Kirk?"

Kirk brightened and started telling her about the sci-fi books he had gotten into. "It's a new gen-ree for me, but I like it."

"Gen-ree?" the queen asked. "Do you mean genre? It's pronounced like john-ruh only with a zh sound for the g," the queen explained.

"Oh, you know what I mean," Kirk said in an uncharacteristically **flippant** way.

★ ★ ★ ★ ★ ★ ★ ★ ★ ★

flippant – *rude*

★ ★ ★ ★ ★ ★ ★ ★ ★ ★

"Kirk, I am just trying to help you pronounce words correctly." Kirk nodded and asked to be excused. When he had left the table, the queen tried to get the king's attention. "Did you hear what he was saying?"

"He, who?"

"Kirk, of course!"

"Oh, what was he saying?"

The queen tried to hide her frustration. "He was pronouncing words incorrectly. At first I thought it was just computer talk with cashay."

"There's no cashay in computers. Wait! Did he mean cache? That's pronounced like the word for money — cash. Hm."

"Yes. He mispronounced raspberry, cocoa, and genre, too."

"Are you thinking he needs a speech therapist? You were certainly wrong that I needed an audiologist."

"I don't know," the queen said. "But it wouldn't hurt to have him evaluated."

Later, the queen worked with Screen to find a good speech therapist for Kirk. She arranged for her to come the next day.

After dinner that evening, the queen found Kirk at his computer. She decided to tell him about the therapist.

"What? Why? I don't need a speech therapist," he said, clearly upset.

"It's just that you've been mispronouncing everything, Kirk."

"What? That's hyper bowl. I mispronounced gen-ree, I mean genre. Big deal."

"You mispronounced cache and raspberry and cocoa. And what is a hyper bowl? A bowl that moves around?"

Kirk sighed. "Hyper bowl means exaggerated, as in I don't have a speech problem."

"Oh, you mean **hyperbole**. It's pronounced hi-per-buh-lee, stressing per." Kirk scowled. "Kirk, listen. You'll meet with the speech therapist and if she agrees there is no problem, all will be well." She patted his arm and left him.

★ ★ ★ ★ ★ ★ ★ ★ ★ ★

hyperbole – *exaggeration*

smugly – *arrogantly*

★ ★ ★ ★ ★ ★ ★ ★ ★ ★

The next day when the speech therapist arrived, she tried to make Kirk comfortable. She had him smile and swallow some water. She even watched him eat a piece of raspberry muffin.

She had him say a long list of words and made notes as he did. She asked him if he liked to read. "I love to read!" he said, smiling for the first time.

"That's wonderful! Do you look up new words when you come to them?"

"Of course," he said proudly.

"How about the pronunciation of new words? Or do you just look up definitions?" His facial expression gave her the answer. "Okay. Don't worry. Very normal." She smiled to encourage him. "I'm going to speak with your parents now. It was so nice meeting you." She shook his hand and Kirk told his parents she wanted to meet with them.

The therapist greeted the royal couple and informed them that she had good news. "Kirk does not have a speech disorder."

The king looked at the queen **smugly**. The queen ignored him. "That is good news!" the queen said, relieved. "But what's wrong with him then?"

67

"He lacks dictionary skills."

"What?" the king asked, astonished. "What do you mean?"

"I mean that like many people who read a lot, Kirk doesn't use a dictionary to learn the pronunciation of words. Of course, accurate pronunciation also comes from being read to. But independent readers need to learn pronunciation from the dictionary as well."

"Great grammar! I can't believe we haven't taught him that. We've failed as parents, dear," he said. He bowed his head, ashamed.

"Now that *is* hyperbole," the therapist said, trying not to laugh. "Like I told Kirk, it's normal and easily fixed with some teaching."

The three called Kirk back into the room to explain what they discussed. Kirk felt much better after their talk. When the therapist left, the king asked Luke and Ellen to join them in the library. The king read the guidebook entry on dictionary skills.

Dictionary Skills
Dictionaries give the correct spelling and definitions of words. They also indicate the part of speech (e.g., noun, verb, adjective, adverb). An important skill in using a dictionary is learning the pronunciation of a word. Digital dictionaries often provide audio of correct pronunciations. However, learning some pronunciation symbols is important, too. For example, the pronunciation guide for the word *after* is /ˈaftər/. The stress mark (ˈ) shows that the first syllable in *after* is emphasized or stressed. Emphasis on a syllable is also shown with bold or capital letters. The schwa (ə) sounds like uh in the word *again*. /ˈviZHən/ is the pronunciation guide for the word *vision*.

"If I was having trouble pronouncing words, do you think the guardians could be, too?" Kirk asked.

"I think it's likely," the king answered.

The three English children wrote a mission they called Dictionary Skills.

"It's no hyper bowl to call this an important mission," Kirk said. When his mother looked concerned, he grinned. "Just kidding!"

What does *hyperbole* mean?

Why did the queen think Kirk had a speech disorder?

How can a dictionary help with learning correct pronunciation?

Chapter 14

The day of the king's birthday party had arrived. The queen was more excited about his birthday than she had ever been for her own. She hoped he would be thrilled with the surprise she had planned.

Ellen had wanted to be in on the plans as well. She wasn't able to help make the cake, which was going to be large enough to serve a crowd. But she had helped choose the decorations.

The queen had invited over a hundred people. Her husband loved talking to people. She was more **reserved**, but she was still looking forward to it. She had not seen some of the guests in months.

★ ★ ★ ★ ★ ★ ★ ★ ★ ★

reserved – *quiet*

★ ★ ★ ★ ★ ★ ★ ★ ★ ★

Ellen and the queen checked in with the kitchen staff to see how the meal preparation was going. Cook was obviously stressed. It was important to her that the party be a success. The queen tried to reassure her. "It smells heavenly. And you know the king loves everything you make."

Cook was momentarily cheered. "Thank you, Your Highness."

The two ladies hoped to peek at the cake but were told that the decorator was still working on it.

The two then left to see how the decorations were coming. A large banner was hung and the grand hall was filled with colorful balloons. "It looks so festive!" Ellen exclaimed.

"It does, doesn't it?" the queen said, beaming. She walked around and reached out to straighten a few tablecloths and decorations. At the head table, she took in the whole view and pronounced it perfect. Ellen again agreed.

As the king was getting ready for guests, he downplayed his excitement. "I suppose I should wear my best suit tonight unless you think I can go in casual clothes." He smirked as the queen playfully poked him.

"I know you're excited. You can't fool me!" she replied.

"I am looking forward to seeing some of our friends who haven't been around in a while," he said.

"Oh, me, too! It will be good to visit."

"So what entertainment do you have planned?" the king asked.

"That's a surprise!" the queen teased. "I really think you're going to enjoy it, though."

"I know I will," the king said **affectionately**. "And there will be food, right? What more do we need?"

★ ★ ★ ★ ★ ★ ★ ★ ★ ★

affectionately – *lovingly*

befitting – *appropriate to*

★ ★ ★ ★ ★ ★ ★ ★ ★ ★

Servants made sure that all the guests were in the grand hall in time for the king and queen's entrance. The guests were dressed in fine clothes **befitting** the occasion. All applauded when a herald announced the entrance of the king and queen. The king stood a little straighter and hoped his guests would think he was aging well.

"Welcome, welcome, everyone!" he called out. "Please be seated."

The meal was served. The guests could be heard murmuring their appreciation for the food. Reports of their praise were given to Cook, who nearly collapsed with relief.

The master of ceremonies got the guests' attention. He told a corny joke to start the entertainment. Everyone was in a good mood and laughed authentically. "Now then," he began. "It is my privilege to introduce the entertainer for the evening. Please welcome the Magnificent Magic E!"

The guests oohed and aahed as the magician walked to the head table. The king made it clear to his wife that he was delighted and she rejoiced inwardly.

"Your Majesty!" the magician said, bowing to the king. "Would you do me the honor of assisting me?" The crowd applauded and cheered as the king made his way to the magician's side. The Magnificent Magic E removed something from his sleeve and held it in front of him. "What am I holding, Your Majesty?"

"Why that's an e," he answered, smiling for the crowd.

71

"Indeed it is." The magician removed his hat and held it out to the king. "Now examine this hat thoroughly if you would. Be certain there are no trick compartments in it. Nothing out of the ordinary."

The king obeyed and said that it looked like a normal hat to him.

"Very well then. I'm going to put this e into the hat, all right?" The king nodded. The Magnificent Magic E removed another letter from his sleeve and asked the king to identify it.

"That, sir, is an *a*," the king answered, having fun with his part of the show.

"Very well. I will add this to the hat as well." The magician removed an i, o, u, and y from his sleeve in turn and added them to the hat. "Now then, I have added an e, a, i, o, u, and y to the hat."

A woman walked toward the magician and king, carrying a rabbit in a cage. The magician removed the rabbit and said, "This is my rabbit, Vowel. I call him Vowel because instead of carrots, he eats vowels." He put the rabbit into his hat and covered the hat with a cloth the assistant handed to him. "He can quickly make these letters disappear."

He withdrew a wand from his sleeve and waved it over the hat. "A-e-i-o-u. Alli kazam, alli kazoo," he said dramatically. When he pulled the cloth off the hat, there was no sign of the rabbit. The guests gasped. "Your Majesty, would you care to check the hat?" he asked.

The king felt inside of the hat and found no sign of the rabbit or letters. "They've disappeared!" he announced to the crowd cheerfully.

"Thank you so much for assisting me. Let's show our king some appreciation!" he said. When the king had returned to his seat, the Magnificent Magic E continued. "Making a rabbit and a few letters disappear is one thing. But what if I could make a man disappear? I know some of you are thinking about who you could volunteer to help me." The crowd snickered. "But I'm afraid I can't do you that favor. Instead, I'm going to ask my lovely assistant to bring me my magic cloak." When she handed it to him, he put it on. He then asked her to hand him his hat. As soon as it touched his head, there seemed to be a small explosion at the spot where he stood. When the smoke cleared, his cloak and hat lay on the floor. But he was gone!

The crowd stood and looked around the room to see if they could spot him. When they could not, they applauded him eagerly. The king was astonished and leaned over to tell his wife what an excellent magician she had hired.

The king's birthday cake was brought to the head table. Its candles were already lit. The king's face decorated one side of the cake. The king was just about to compliment the queen on the cake when he noticed the writing. "HPP BRTHD!" it read. The king's eyes grew wide. He decided not to mention it and spoil the queen's happiness.

"Make a wish!" many in attendance called out. The king thought for a moment and then blew out the candles. He called for the cake to be served to the guests immediately.

"Oh, let's let the guests see it first," the queen objected. "The decorator did a marvelous job making the cake look like you."

"Uh," the king stammered. "I love the cake. But there is a problem with the writing on it."

"What?" the queen shrieked. "Let me see!" When she saw how 'Happy Birthday' was written, she was mortified. "It's ruined!"

"It's not ruined, dear. Is it my favorite cake dough?"

"Of course."

"Then it will be wonderful. Let's just have it served and no one will see the writing. You've already outdone yourself with the entertainment."

The queen seemed satisfied with the king's plan. As she turned to ask for the cake to be cut, she gasped. A banner that had once read 'HAPPY BIRTHDAY' now read 'HPP BRTHD.' Careful not to point, she told her husband to look at the banner. "That is not what it said when I checked it this morning."

The king sighed. "The Gremlin is up to something again. But let's enjoy the rest of the party. We'll investigate later." The queen agreed and they did have a wonderful time talking with their friends.

After everyone had left, the royal couple informed the children what they had seen on the cake and banner. Luke showed the king his tablet. "I wasn't going to tell you. I didn't want to spoil your birthday. But the vowels are definitely gone."

"How is that possible?" the king asked.

"I did some research on it, Father," Kirk said. "The vowels are missing from planet Spelling. There are no clues to their whereabouts."

"Why would the Gremlin want the vowels?" Ellen asked.

"Because spelling is impossible without them," the king explained. "They're part of a number of spelling rules." He requested the guidebook be brought to him and he read the entry on spelling rules aloud.

Spelling Rules
There are words in the English language that don't follow spelling rules. But learning spelling rules can improve spelling.

One spelling rule is sometimes called Magic E. A word or syllable that has the vowel-consonant-e pattern usually has a long vowel sound. The e is silent. For example, cake, plate, shame.

A second common spelling rule is that every syllable contains a vowel. For example, table, gym, everything .

A third common spelling rule is i before e except after c or when ei says /ay/ as in neighbor and weigh. For example, friend, believe, relief.

A fourth common spelling rule is that c makes the /s/ sound when followed by e, i, or y. For example, nice, city, cynic.

A fifth common spelling rule is to double final consonants in one-syllable, short-vowel words that end in f, l, s, or z. For example, Gliding from a <u>cliff</u> is <u>bliss</u> and a <u>buzz</u> but it requires <u>skill</u>.

"There are more rules, of course, but it's late," the king said.

"All the rules you read need vowels!" Ellen said.

"They do. We have to get the vowels back or everything will be misspelled," the king said.

"When we get them back, we still have a problem," Luke said sadly. When his family asked him to explain, he said, "I didn't know those spelling rules. It seems like so much to remember!"

"It is if you try to learn them all at once. But if you learn a few every week, you can really improve your spelling," the king said.

"I'm in!" Luke said. "I would love to have the guardians learn them with me."

"Great idea, Luke. Now if we just had an idea for getting the vowels back," the king said.

"I have one!" Ellen exclaimed. "The guardians can do it."

The king was confident his children could handle the problem, so he went to bed. Kirk, Luke, and Ellen created a mission called Spelling Rules which would be sent out first thing in the morning.

What does it mean that the queen is more *reserved*?

What do you think the king's favorite cake dough is?

Three letters were missing from the king's cake. What are they?

Unit III: Adventures in Grammar

Chapter 15

The three English children were so excited. In a few days, they would be leaving for Grammar Camp. They would have a whole week to spend in the wilderness with some of their fellow guardians.

Kirk was most excited about seeing some of the friends who joined him at camp every year. Ellen was most excited about horseback riding. And Luke was just excited. It would be the first year he was old enough to attend. His siblings enjoyed telling him about the food, camp chores, and campfire activities.

The king and queen prepared for bed one night that week and discussed camp. They agreed it would feel strange not to have any of their three children home. "We should do something romantic," the queen mused. "We could have a candlelight dinner outside, just the two of us."

"It doesn't matter where we have dinner. It will just be the two of us," the king said.

The queen sighed. Then she had an idea. "We could go away, too! Wouldn't it be lovely to spend the week at the lake?"

The king's expression indicated that he didn't think it would be lovely. "Well—"

"Please, dear. It would mean so much to me," she pleaded.

The king smiled, giving in. "If it will make you happy, then by all means we'll go."

The queen was ecstatic and began chattering about everything she needed to do to get ready for the lake while the king fell asleep.

The next morning, the children ate their breakfasts quickly. They announced that they needed to start packing. The queen had made sure that each of them had a copy of their packing list. She wanted them to be responsible. Besides, it was really part of the fun of camp.

When the three of them left the dining room, the queen decided to start researching the lake trip. She didn't have much time and she hoped she could find the perfect place to stay. She asked Screen to display the places with the **amenities** she was looking for. She was considering them when Kirk appeared, needing her help.

★ ★ ★ ★ ★ ★ ★ ★ ★ ★

amenities – *services*

★ ★ ★ ★ ★ ★ ★ ★ ★ ★

"Yes, dear? Oh, look at this delightful cabin, Kirk. I think your father would like this one, don't you?"

Kirk nodded. "I can't find m—. I can't find m—." He was getting frustrated.

"You can't find what, dear? Slow down."

"I can't find m—." He removed his communicator and pointed to the compass listed on his packing list. "Compass."

"Oh, y—, y— compass. Goodness. Now I'm talking too fast."

"Do you know where it is?" Kirk asked.

"Yes, I do. I had it put in the observatory."

Kirk didn't want to criticize his mother for moving his compass, so he just said thank you. Then he left to look for it.

The queen returned her attention to her lake trip research. "We could rent a boat!" she squealed. "But what kind of boat?" She asked Screen to list the options. While she was waiting, Ellen appeared.

"Mother, do you know where m-, m-?" she started.

"Ellen, I know you're excited, but slow down."

"Okay." Ellen agreed that she was talking fast. "I can't find m-, m-. Ugh!" She stopped herself. "Jeans! I need jeans so I can ride horses this week."

"Ohh, yes. Those would be with the fall and winter clothing."

"And where would I find that?"

The queen reluctantly agreed to help Ellen find her jeans. Ellen was relieved when they found them in storage. "You better try them on. You've grown!" They agreed that the jeans still fit.

Ellen noticed a long-sleeved shirt in the closet. "Should I bring m—, m—? Should I bring this, too? It does get chilly at night."

"Yes, and it will keep you from getting bitten by mosquitoes, too."

Ellen and the queen were leaving the storage area when Luke found them. "Mother, I can't find m—, m—." Ellen and the queen both told him to slow down. "I can't find m—, m—. The camp t-shirt I got. I can't find it!" He seemed near tears.

"Don't worry," the queen said, hugging him. "When the shirts came, I put them all in one place. They're next to ou-, ou-. Okay, I'm not talking fast, but I'm stuttering. Something is wrong."

She and the children agreed they needed to find Kirk and the king so they could help. They explained their stuttering problem and Kirk agreed that it was a concern. "I don't seem to be stuttering," the king said.

"We don't stutter all the time. It happened when we were talking about the children—, the children—. See, it's happening again!" the queen said.

"Hm. I wonder if the Gremlin is behind this," the king said. He asked Screen to look for any major news stories that could explain what was happening.

They didn't find anything, so they started searching for local news. There were no headlines, so the queen began reading the **obituaries**. "Oh, look, dear, the word *groak* has died. How sad," she said.

★ ★ ★ ★ ★ ★ ★ ★ ★

obituaries – *death announcements*

★ ★ ★ ★ ★ ★ ★ ★ ★

"What does that mean again?" the king asked.

"It says here that it means to stare at someone while they eat. You hope you'll be asked to eat, too," the queen answered.

"Comet groaks all the time!" Luke said, laughing. The queen hushed him and said it wasn't respectful to joke about a dead word.

The king asked to see crime news for the galaxy. There were speeding tickets and minor thefts reported. But there was a crime listing that was repeated multiple times. The word *your* was served a **restraining** order for being possessive. So was the word *their*. The words *my* and *our* were listed as well. When the queen tried to say them, she was unable to.

★ ★ ★ ★ ★ ★ ★ ★ ★

restraining – *limiting*

★ ★ ★ ★ ★ ★ ★ ★ ★

"Why, these are possessive pronouns. We need them. It's not a crime to be possessive," the king declared.

"But it is possible to be too possessive, isn't it?" the queen asked.

"Of course, but words can't be too possessive." The king was ready to stop reading when the queen pointed out another crime.

A punctuation mark had been arrested for being an imposter. It pretended to be something it wasn't, the report read. "Why in the galaxy would they think this apostrophe was an imposter?" the king said, pointing at its picture. "Punctuation marks don't fake their identity," the king said, shaking his head.

"Wait. You said it's an apostrophe?" Kirk asked. "This report is calling it an impostrophe."

"There's no such thing!" the king exclaimed. Then he sighed. "All right, we have work to do." He requested that the guidebook be brought to him. When it was, he read them the entry on possessive nouns and pronouns.

Possessive Nouns and Pronouns
Possessive nouns and pronouns show ownership. **Possessive nouns are created by adding an apostrophe + an s ('s) to the end of the noun.** the throne belonging to the king = king's throne the bone belonging to Comet = Comet's bone **The exception to this rule is for plural nouns (showing more than one) that already end in s. In this case, only the apostrophe is added to the end of the word.**

the leader belonging to the aliens – aliens' leader

the galaxy belonging to the stars = the stars' galaxy

<u>The apostrophe goes after the owner or owners</u>. *The childrens' books* is incorrect because the books don't belong to the childrens. Ask who the item belongs to and add the apostrophe to that. Include an **s** if the owner is singular. *The princess's shoe* is correct. There is only one princess and the shoe belongs to her. Princess is singular, so **'s** is added. *The princesses' shoes* is also correct. The shoes belong to the princesses. Princesses is plural and ends in s. Only an apostrophe is added.

Possessive pronouns include its, my, mine, your, yours, his, her, hers, our, ours, their, theirs, and whose. <u>Possessive prononouns do not have apostrophes</u>. It's is a contraction for *it is* and is not a possessive pronoun.

"What are we going to do about the apostrophe? We need it!" Ellen said.

"Don't forget the possessive pronouns. I need m—, m—. I need them," Luke said.

"Yeah, it's making it awfully hard to pack for camp without them," Kirk agreed.

The king had an idea. "I think I can get the judge to release the apostrophe and drop the restraining orders. But I'll need the guardians' help."

He didn't have to say more. The guardians began work on a mission called Possessive Nouns and Pronouns right away. They hoped this latest crisis could be cleared up in time for Grammar Camp.

What word was listed in the *obituaries*?

Why couldn't the royal family use possessive nouns or pronouns?

In the phrase *childrens luggage*, does the apostrophe (') go before or after the s in childrens?

Chapter 16

The king was in his study, working on his autobiography when the queen knocked on his door. He seemed delighted that she was there and asked her to listen to the latest story he had written.

"Oh, dear, the children will love that story, truly," she said, her eyes shining.

"You're such an encourager," the king said lovingly. The queen blushed a bit. "Did you need something? Is that why you came looking for me?"

"I don't need anything. I was just going to tell you that planet Sentence is hosting a motivational speaker tonight. I wondered if you would want to go."

"Ohh," the king said, looking disappointed. "You know that isn't my favorite thing. I don't enjoy listening to speakers. They always go on too long." He saw his wife's **countenance** fall. He stood up and took her hand. "I know you'd love it, though. Would you be too disappointed if I didn't go?"

★ ★ ★ ★ ★ ★ ★ ★ ★ ★

countenance – *face*

★ ★ ★ ★ ★ ★ ★ ★ ★ ★

The queen did look disappointed, but she said, "No. I could go by myself. That's fine. I'm sure you want to get some writing done."

"You're the best," the king said, hugging her. "You can tell me all about it."

"Yes," the queen said, without much enthusiasm.

When the queen left the study, she decided to watch some videos of the speaker. She was sure that would get her looking forward to seeing him in person and it did. "He's so inspiring," she murmured. She purchased a ticket and decided not to let her husband's absence bring her down. She would enjoy the talk.

As she got ready to go that evening, she hoped she wouldn't be too **conspicuous**. It wouldn't do for anyone to see that the queen was attending alone. She had the idea that she could go **incognito**. She put on a wig and

★ ★ ★ ★ ★ ★ ★ ★ ★ ★

conspicuous – *visible*

incognito – *disguised*

★ ★ ★ ★ ★ ★ ★ ★ ★ ★

glasses and giggled at herself in the mirror. She had to dig through her closet to find casual clothing that wouldn't give her away.

She finished putting together her disguise. Then she used the spaceporter to make a quick exit. She didn't want anyone to see her dressed that way.

She arrived on planet Sentence outside the theater. She noticed that her heart was pounding. She was on an exciting adventure! She handed her ticket to the attendant and made her way to her seat. She was thrilled to have a seat in the front row. There were advantages to attending alone, she told herself.

There was great excitement as more attendees took their seats and waited for the speaker to begin. When the emcee for the evening took the stage, there was thunderous applause. People mistook him for the man they had paid to see. He seemed used to that reaction. He smiled broadly and introduced the speaker of the night. When the real speaker appeared on stage, everyone was on their feet, applauding.

When he started talking, the queen couldn't take her eyes off him. He seemed to be talking about her. She wanted to remember every word.

"You're a helper," he said. "You do everything you can to take care of your family. You put them first. And other people, too." And that's a good thing. That's what we're taught to do." He stopped and seemed to be looking straight at the queen. "But what about you? When is it time for your dreams?"

"Yes!" the queen responded. "What about me?" She said it out loud, forgetting where she was.

"No one will respect you until you respect you," he continued.

"That's right!" the queen said loudly. No one noticed because others in the theater were saying the same thing.

"If you don't take care of you, who will?" he asked.

"No one," the queen and many in the audience responded.

"I met some words when I arrived on planet Sentence who needed to hear this message tonight. I've asked them to come on stage with me." The words *am, is, are, were, was, have, had, do, did, can, will, could*, *would*, and *should* joined him on stage. He read them one by one and said, "You guys are helpers, right?" The words appeared to blink in agreement. "That's wonderful. Can we give them a round of applause?" The crowd clapped.

"We appreciate you," the speaker continued. "But when is it your time?" The words blinked and shifted from foot to foot. "I know it's uncomfortable when you're a helper to think about yourself. But that's why I'm going to help you." He patted one of the words. "I'm going to give all of you free tuition to my Make Your Dream Happen Academy."

The audience seemed impressed with the speaker's generosity and applauded appreciatively. "My staff is going to take you there now." Two people appeared, directing the words off stage and waving to the crowd.

"Now what about you?" he asked the audience. "Isn't it time for you? I have staff members who will be handing out invitations to join me in the Make Your Dream Happen Academy."

The queen couldn't wait to get her invitation. When she did, she was pretty surprised by the cost. She heard others around her saying the same. "I really want to do it, though," the queen said to herself. "I would need to ask my husband first."

The speaker interrupted her thoughts. "Whose permission do you need to do what's best for you? Right now you're probably thinking, 'This is a lot of money. I better ask my husband, my wife, my parents, my boss, my neighbor—" He snickered. "'I have to get permission to live my dream,' you're thinking. No, you don't! If you're ready to change your life and stop being more than someone else's helper, join one of my staff members. They are waiting for you outside the back doors."

The queen trembled as she tried to decide what to do. Around her, she heard people proclaiming, "I'm going for it!"

She smiled and said, "Me, too." She made her way to the back of the theater and to what she hoped would be a new way of life.

Back at the castle, Kirk was ready to turn in for the night when he realized he hadn't seen his mother. He found his father in the study and asked about her. The king seemed surprised by the lateness of the hour. But he reassured Kirk that these events always run late. "Probably waiting for an autograph," he said, winking.

Kirk went to bed and an hour later, when she still hadn't returned, the king started to worry. He messaged her communicator: "Coming home soon?" When there was no response for fifteen minutes, he decided to investigate. Maybe the event had started late and she had her communicator off, he thought.

"Screen," the king said, "did the motivational speaker on planet Sentence begin on time tonight?"

"Yes, Your Majesty," was the reply.

"Is traffic still backed up?"

"No, Sire. The theater traffic is gone."

The king felt sick. "Has there been any kind of accident?" When the answer was no, the king contacted security on planet Sentence directly. The man in charge had no information on the whereabouts of the queen. The king asked him to keep the missing person report from the media and he agreed.

The king didn't sleep all night. When Kirk asked him if his mother had gotten home, the king fought back tears to say no.

"— you call security?" Kirk asked. The king nodded. "— you — Screen help?"

"I — Screen help," the king answered. His eyes grew wide. "I — not say some words."

Kirk nodded. "Which words? We — know which words."

"Yes. Screen, I need a report on the speaker last night. What — he say?"

"Certainly," Screen answered. Screen displayed a news story on the speech. A reporter stood in front of the darkened theater.

"The highlight of the night was when a large group of words was given free tuition to Make Your Dream Come True Academy. Here's a clip." The video showed the words on stage with the speaker.

"They — helping verbs!" the king exclaimed.

The reporter continued. "Hundreds of people signed up for the academy despite the high tuition." The camera showed lines of people waiting to pay.

"Wait!" the king yelled."Pause the video."

"What — it?" Kirk asked.

"It — your mother," he said, pointing.

Kirk argued at first, but as he continued to stare at the screen, he admitted that it had to be her. "What –- we do?"

"We go get her," the king said.

"What about the helping verbs?"

"Them, too. We need the guardians' help, Kirk. Look up helping verbs in the guidebook. Tell Ellen and Luke what — happening."

The three English children read about helping verbs in the guidebook.

Helping Verbs
Helping verbs give more information about the main verb, often about when action occurred. Helping verbs include forms of: **to be:** am, is, are, was, were, be, being, been **to have:** have, has, had **to do:** do, does, did, done **conditionals:** could, should, would, can, shall, will, may, might, must For example, <u>The girl was shopping with her mother</u>. The helping verb <u>was</u> shows that the main verb <u>shopping</u> occurred in the past.

They knew they needed the guardians to complete the Helping Verbs mission. But they were most concerned about getting their mother home.

What does it mean that the queen's *"countenance fell"*?

What helping verb was missing?: "I –- not say some words."

Why couldn't Kirk and the king say helping verbs?

Chapter 17

"Your mother and I have a big surprise for you!" the king announced. The queen had asked him to save the surprise, but he couldn't help himself. He wanted to tell the children right away.

He was met with a chorus of "what is it?" He relished the moment. With a dramatic pause, he announced that the whole family would be going to Tomorrow Universe. It was the theme park that the whole galaxy had been talking about.

"No way!" Luke shrieked.

"Yes way!" the queen said, laughing.

The three children celebrated and finally thought to ask when they would be going.

"In two weeks," the queen said. She looked at her husband as if to say she thought that was too long to make them wait.

"Two weeks," Ellen said. "That's just enough time to pack."

The queen laughed again. "Before you pack, we are going to want to read all about it." She handed the kids a Tomorrow Universe guide. "This will help you decide what you want to see most."

"I want to see all of it!" Luke declared.

The king and queen both laughed.

"Don't you have something to say?" the queen reminded her children.

"Thank you, Father!" they said, hugging him.

"You are welcome!" he said, beaming. He whispered to the queen, "I'm glad I told them now."

A week later, he wasn't as glad he had told them. His children repeatedly asked him how many days were left until their trip. They couldn't concentrate, either. But he understood. It was a very exciting trip. He was looking forward to it, too.

When their **departure** day arrived, he was just as excited as his children. He had one more surprise for all of them. They were going to take a space shuttle to Tomorrow Universe. None of them had ever ridden in a shuttle before. It would give them a chance to see their entire galaxy.

★ ★ ★ ★ ★ ★ ★ ★ ★ ★

departure – *leaving*

★ ★ ★ ★ ★ ★ ★ ★ ★ ★

He let everyone think they were taking the spaceporter until the last minute. Then he announced that they would be launching from the Galactic Space Center. The children celebrated. The queen asked him how in the galaxy he had kept it a secret. He shrugged and put his arm around his wife. "Are you excited?" he asked her.

"Definitely! I just hope I won't be spacesick."

"You will be fine on this ship. Promise," he reassured her.

Once on the ship, the queen was pleasantly surprised by the smooth ride. "It isn't bad at all," she admitted.

"Told you so," the king smirked.

Kirk, Luke, and Ellen were more preoccupied with the drinks and snacks than the king had expected. He kept drawing their attention to the views out the large windows. Eventually, he became interested in the snacks, too.

The shuttle landed on the moon that was home to Tomorrow Universe. The whole family thanked the captain for flying them. He seemed genuinely happy to do it.

From the spaceport, the family traveled by spacecopter to the resort. The family had rented private quarters. Kirk was excited to see what their rooms would look like. The guide had had pictures of standard rooms, but he knew the royal family would stay in a suite. What kind of cool, futuristic **lodging** would it be? What advanced technology would it have?

★ ★ ★ ★ ★ ★ ★ ★ ★ ★

lodging – *room*

★ ★ ★ ★ ★ ★ ★ ★ ★ ★

A porter had their luggage and opened the door for them. Kirk couldn't believe the décor. "It's a log cabin!" he exclaimed.

Ellen and the queen began discussing sleeping arrangements. Luke declared it cool. The king was most interested in the view of the park from their windows. "It's incredible, isn't it?"

Kirk didn't answer at first as he continued to try to make sense of his surroundings. "This isn't a Tomorrow Universe room. This is a historical room." He was obviously disappointed.

"Kirk, not everything in Tomorrow Universe is going to be future-focused."

"It's not?"

"No. There will probably be a lot of historical rides and shows."

"That's weird."

"Why is that weird? History can be every bit as exciting as the future."

"I know. It's just that—they didn't show anything like this in the guide."

"Oh. Kirk, I bet your guide wasn't updated. They add new attractions to this resort all the time." When Kirk still seemed disappointed, the king said, "Kirk, don't worry. This is the happiest place in the universe."

Kirk had to smile at that. "You're right. It just isn't what I expected. But it is pretty neat. I've never slept in a log cabin before."

"That's right! Neither have I," the king agreed. "Let's get some sleep so we can be all be well rested in the park tomorrow."

The next morning, everyone was up early. This time, no one was very interested in food. Everyone wanted to get to the park. The queen had a list of places they wanted to see on their first day. The king had made it clear that they wouldn't be skipping lines because they were royalty. He didn't think that was fair. Besides, he said it would teach them all patience.

But in the line for the first ride, he muttered that the decision had been a mistake. The queen tried to keep him from losing his temper. She kept pointing out things displayed on the walls for them to read.

"Look at this old map of the galaxy, dear. Isn't it funny that the moon that we're on wasn't even on the map?" she said.

"Yes, yes, that's funny," the king grumbled.

Kirk recognized his father's foul mood but couldn't help himself. He asked, "Don't you think it's strange that they have so much historical stuff here?"

"No. They're probably just showing you the old ways first. That way the ways of tomorrow will seem that much more amazing," the king answered.

That satisfied Kirk. He couldn't wait to experience the ride they were in line for. But when they finally reached the boarding area, Kirk was more confused than ever. They were going to be riding in what looked like mining cars. As they were carried along, a tour guide's voice explained the history of mining. Animatronic miners hammered on the walls as the cars traveled by.

"That was fascinating!" the king declared when the ride was over. "Didn't you think so, Kirk?"

Kirk tried to hide his discontent so he wouldn't upset his father. "Yes, yes. Very interesting."

The king wasn't fooled. "Kirk, there are going to be plenty of futuristic rides and exhibits in this park." He insisted that Kirk give him a smile, which he genuinely did. Kirk figured his father had to be right. It was Tomorrow Universe after all.

But the next attraction they visited was the same. It demonstrated how native peoples had once lived all over the galaxy. Kirk was hopeful that the transportation exhibit would be more exciting. He convinced the rest of his family to go there next.

Kirk expected new kinds of space vehicles and a promise of even faster spaceporting. Instead, the only vehicles on display were old cars, planes, and motorcycles. Luke seemed to enjoy them. He pretended he was driving and flying. Luke especially loved the simulator which allowed you to feel like you were flying an old plane. That was okay, but Kirk couldn't hide his frustration any longer.

The king, who was tired, snapped at Kirk. "I have spent a lot of time and money on this trip, Kirk. For you!"

Kirk immediately apologized, but the conflict definitely changed the family's mood.

When the family returned to their quarters and the king and queen were in their room, Kirk knocked on the door. After the king invited him in, Kirk apologized again. "Forgiven," the king said. "I apologize, too. I lost my temper. I thought it would be fine to wait in long lines and it wasn't."

Kirk let him know he understood. "I know I behaved badly, but I really think something is wrong. Nothing in Tomorrow Universe has been about the future. It's all about the past."

The king considered what Kirk said for a moment. "You know, you're right. I kept thinking that the historical attractions would lead to futuristic ones. But they didn't. I just didn't want to think that the Gremlin could be causing problems again. I'm on vacation," the king said, sighing.

"I know. I'm sorry," Kirk said.

"We can't do anything about it tonight. We w—, w—. See? I'm exhausted. Must sleep."

Kirk let his father get to sleep. But he decided to do a little research on his own. He used his portable screen to look for anything that could explain why Tomorrow Universe was such a letdown.

A search for information on Tomorrow Universe turned up nothing. There were also no news stories of any sort to explain it. Kirk did a general search for *tomorrow*. That also showed nothing. But when he searched for future, something interesting appeared. It was a **documentary** about how verbs traveled to planet Sentence. They had to take one of three routes: past, present, or future.

★ ★ ★ ★ ★ ★ ★ ★ ★ ★

documentary – *film*

★ ★ ★ ★ ★ ★ ★ ★ ★ ★

The camera crew followed a verb on the past route. It looked very much like Tomorrow Universe – full of old things. The present route looked a little old. But that's because the documentary had been made a couple of decades before. The future route looked almost exactly like what Kirk had thought Tomorrow Universe would look like.

There was something at the beginning of the video that bothered Kirk. He reversed it until he saw it. There were three simple signs showing verbs which route to take. What if the Gremlin had switched the signs?

The next morning, Kirk shared his theory. The king was upset. "We made it entirely too easy for the Gremlin to tamper with these signs."

"But why did he? Why does he care about Tomorrow Universe?" Kirk asked.

"Kirk, this is much bigger than Tomorrow Universe. I need to explain it to you. Oh, no," he groaned. "I don't have the guidebook."

"I brought it!" the queen interjected. "I wanted to be prepared for everything."

The king hugged her appreciatively and read the entry on verb tenses to all three children.

Verb Tenses
There are three main verb tenses that show when something occurred. **Present tense** shows that something is happening now. Present tense helping verbs include *is, am,* and *are*. Combined with the **-ing** form of the verb, they show present tense. He is complaining. They are traveling. Present tense verbs can also end in –s for singular subjects and have no ending for plural subjects. He complains. They travel. **Past tense verbs** show that something has already occurred. They end in –d or –ed. He complained. They traveled. **Future tense verbs** show that something will happen in the future. *Will* or *shall* are used in the future tense. He will complain. They will travel.

"I see why you said it's a bigger problem than Tomorrow Universe," Kirk said.

"Can we just have someone switch the signs back?" Luke asked.

"No," Ellen said. "Because there are already verbs on the wrong route, right, Father?"

"That's right. We need the guardians to help put them on the right path," the king said.

"Can we fix it fast enough that we can still enjoy Tomorrow Universe the way it is supposed to be?" Kirk asked.

"I can't say we w—, but I can say we can," the king said.

Kirk, Luke, and Ellen sent out an emergency mission called Verb Tenses.

What does *lodging* mean?

The king said, "I can't say we w—, but I can say we can." What word couldn't he say?

Why wasn't Tomorrow Universe what Kirk expected?

Chapter 18

The English kids cheered when the queen announced that they would be vacationing in Yesterland. Their father had made the decision because their trip to Tomorrow Universe had been shortened.

Ellen was especially excited. She loved old-fashioned dresses and antiques.

"The old days were a slower time. I'm looking forward to a relaxing trip. Maybe we should take a break from technology. What do you think? It might be good for us," the king said. Everyone looked very reluctant. "Okay. We'll think about it, though, right?" The queen and the kids murmured that they would, but they hoped he would forget about it.

The queen asked Screen to show the children what they could expect at Yesterland. They saw craftsmen making candles, pulling taffy, and blowing glass. Kirk was **intrigued** by the blacksmiths. Ellen loved the quilting, and Luke was eager to ride the log flume. "This will be so much fun," the queen declared. Secretly, she was a little worried. It seemed like something always got in the way of their plans. She hoped this would truly be a relaxing vacation.

★ ★ ★ ★ ★ ★ ★ ★ ★ ★

intrigued – *interested*

mortified – *horrified*

★ ★ ★ ★ ★ ★ ★ ★ ★ ★

The king insisted on taking the horse and carriage to Yesterland. The queen was **mortified**. "It will take us all day to get there!"

"But dear, we want to experience life as they did in the past, don't we?"

The queen wanted to say no, but she didn't want to start the vacation with an argument. She sighed and got into the carriage. The children began playing games on their tablets immediately. The king said, "I thought we agreed to leave those behind." When the children said they didn't remember him saying they had to, he said they

94

needed to be put away. "We're going to have fun the old-fashioned way."

"Like what?" Luke asked.

"Like let's play the ABC game. As we travel, we find words that begin with each letter of the alphabet in order. I'll start. Look! There's a sign for the Acme Corporation. We have an A," the king said.

Kirk said, "There's a billboard for Bank of Grammar Galaxy. So that's B."

The family found themselves entertained by the game for quite a while. When Luke asked where they would be eating, the queen shared a surprise. "I asked Cook to prepare us a picnic lunch. We're really doing things like they used to."

"That's fine," Luke said, "as long as we can use a real restroom." The king and queen laughed.

"We won't be that extreme," the king said.

After lunch, the family passed the time by telling stories. Someone would start and the next family member would share the next part of the story. They told several stories that way. Then the children wanted to know when they would arrive at Yesterland. The king would only answer, "Before the sun sets."

All three children wanted to complain, but they knew better. It was hard to leave their electronic devices in their bags. They did stop to stretch their legs and get something to drink. "Imagine if it were really cold or extremely hot and we were traveling this way. We are riding in the open air for fun, but in times past, they had to," the king reminded them.

Ellen knew she shouldn't complain. But she found riding in the carriage all day really uncomfortable. She was thrilled when they arrived at the entrance to Yesterland.

The greeters were dressed in clothing that their mother said was from the Victorian age. Ellen thought their outfits were beautiful. Luke thought they looked too hot to wear.

The family was pleased with their accommodations, with one exception: there was no electricity. Oil lamps were used for lighting and the king got his wish after all. There was no way to charge their electronics.

The three children didn't care. After a light supper in the resort's restaurant, the children went straight to bed.

The next morning, they were up with the sun and eager to explore

Yesterland. They checked the schedule so they wouldn't miss anything. After several hours of leisurely strolling through the park, the queen relaxed. She told herself she was silly to think something would go wrong. It was a perfectly marvelous vacation.

Luke interrupted her thoughts, chattering excitedly. "We seed the glass blowers, Mother. They blowed a vase for us!"

"Just because you're excited doesn't mean you can forget your grammar." The queen looked around nervously, hoping no one had heard him.

"We buyed it for you, but it breaked. I'm so sorry, Mother. I should have beed more careful," Luke said sorrowfully.

"Be careful of your grammar!" she corrected him. "But it's all right. I know you feeled bad." The queen was shocked by what she'd said. "I mean, I mean, it's all right."

The queen decided that she was **dehydrated** and suggested they get something to drink. Luke remembered seeing a freshly-squeezed lemonade stand. The royal family walked to it and purchased three lemonades to share.

★ ★ ★ ★ ★ ★ ★ ★ ★ ★

dehydrated – *thirsty*

★ ★ ★ ★ ★ ★ ★ ★ ★ ★

When Ellen asked to have more from the cup Luke held, he said, "I already drinked it all."

The queen gasped. "Dear," she said, "there's something wrong with Luke's grammar. He sayed drinked." The queen was terrified by what had come out of her mouth.

"I understanded you, but you speaked strangely," the king said. He groaned. "The Gremlin must be up to something."

When Kirk asked his father what he planned to do, the king looked alarmed. "I leaved my communicator at home. There's no Screen here."

"I'll go back with you, Father," Kirk offered.

"That's so mature of you, Kirk. I hate to interrupt another family vacation, so I will accept your help. Your mother and siblings can stay here. I hope we can fix this crisis quickly."

The king and Kirk were flown home in a space taxi. They wasted no time getting Screen to help them. "We flyed here as quickly as we could," the king said.

"Flyed?" Screen asked. "This must be the result of the Anti-Discrimination Act."

"What act? Where?" the king asked.

Screen showed a photo of the entry to the Past Tense route. A sign reading "Irregular Verbs Enter Here" had been painted with an X.

"Show me a live feed of the entry to the Past Tense route, please," the king said.

A line of verbs was waiting to receive their stamp to enter. The verb *eat* was stamped with –ed while they watched.

"No!" the king cried.

"What is it, Father?" Kirk asked.

"Irregular verbs do not get an –ed ending. But there's no longer a separate entrance for them to take the Past Tense route. The Gremlin has convinced people that irregular verbs are being treated unfairly if they don't get an –ed ending. That's ridiculous! Kirk, go and read about irregular verbs in the guidebook. We're going to need the guardians' help to get this sorted out."

Kirk read the entry in the library.

Irregular Verbs
Irregular verbs do not form the past tense using –d or –ed. Examples of irregular verbs include: **blow** (blew), **break** (broke), **buy** (bought), **come** (came), **do** (did), **drink** (drank), **eat** (ate), **feel** (felt), **fly** (flew), **give** (gave), **go** (went), **grow** (grew), **leave** (left), **make** (made), **say** (said), **see** (saw), **sing** (sang), **take** (took), **think** (thought), **wear** (wore), and **write** (wrote). The **to be** verbs (am, is, are) are also irregular (was and were are the past tense). Most irregular verbs are learned in conversation.

Kirk created a mission called Irregular Verbs. He hoped they could finish their vacation if the problem were fixed quickly.

What does *intrigued* mean?

Luke said, "We buyed it for you." What should he have said?

Why was the English family misusing irregular verbs?

97

Chapter 19

"Your Majesty!" The butler interrupted the king's dinner. It was very unusual behavior. The king knew immediately that there was an emergency.

"What is it?"

"A category 5 hurricane has hit the coastal regions of the planet."

The king directed Screen to give him an update. **Catastrophic** damage was being reported. Experts predicted that the area would be **uninhabitable** for months.

"What can we do?" the queen asked.

"We'll need to **dispatch** every emergency worker we can spare. But we'll need disaster response teams as well," the king answered. His

★ ★ ★ ★ ★ ★ ★ ★ ★

catastrophic – *disastrous*

uninhabitable– *ruined*

dispatch – *send*

★ ★ ★ ★ ★ ★ ★ ★ ★

expression was serious.

"Is there anything we can do to help?" Kirk asked.

"Yes, but not yet. The situation on the coast will be very dangerous for some time. Excuse me, will you? I need to consult with the council leaders."

The rest of the family watched him go. They knew he would do whatever he could to help the people affected.

In the weeks following the hurricane, the royal family saw news stories about people who had lost their homes and possessions. There were also amazing rescue stories that lifted the family's spirits.

One evening, the family was gathered in the media room, watching the latest on the hurricane. A reporter was interviewing a family whose house had been damaged by flooding. "How are you doing?" he asked them.

"We—, we—," the father started, but his voice was choked with emotion.

"Oh, the poor man," the queen said, tearing up.

The father being interviewed hugged his wife and child. "Just glad we're all okay."

The reporter turned his attention to a woman standing nearby. "You had quite the scare, didn't you?"

"Yes. I was working in my house when the water started rising. I got to the highest part of my house. But the water kept coming. So I climbed out of the window and onto my roof. I didn't know how long I would be there or if I would be swept away. But then this man came by with his boat and rescued me." She pointed to a man standing next to her and then hugged him. The man seemed embarrassed.

"How are you doing now that you've been rescued?" the reporter asked.

"I—. I—." The woman was unable to continue, so the reporter asked her rescuer how he was.

"I—. I—." He shrugged and smiled awkwardly at the camera.

"There just aren't words," the reporter said, ending his broadcast.

"Those people have PTSD," the king said.

"What's that?" Ellen asked.

"It stands for post-traumatic stress disorder. It is what happens to some people when they survive a very stressful situation," he explained. "I don't want you to watch too many of these reports. It's stressful just hearing about it."

"I know what you mean," Luke said. "I saw a story about a family who couldn't find their dog. I—, I—. If he—." Luke buried his face in Comet's fur.

"Your reaction tells me you need to stop watching the news. Agreed?" Luke nodded yes. "My two favorite ladies haven't been watching a lot of this news, right? I know how sensitive you two are," the king said.

"I—. I—," Ellen started. Her shoulders sagged. She couldn't deny that she had been very upset watching the news.

"I—. I—," the queen said. "I need to quit watching, too."

"All right then. I—. I—," the king started.

"Are you upset too, Father? It's okay to be sad. That's what Mother always tells us," Ellen said.

"No, I—, I—. Something—," the king stammered.

"What—? What—?" Kirk asked. He stopped for a moment and his eyes grew wide. "The Gremlin wouldn't have done something now, would he? I'm having trouble speaking."

"Me, too!" the rest of the family chimed in.

"The Gremlin would definitely choose now to attack the galaxy. He knows we are all focused on helping the victims of the hurricane." The king tried to control his temper. He knew he needed to think clearly. "It has to be something on planet Sentence. I can start some sentences, but then I'm stuck. Come to think of it, those people being interviewed for the news did the same thing!"

The king asked Screen to search for news stories that would explain their difficulty talking. When nothing came up, he was frustrated. "I have a feeling that whatever the Gremlin has done didn't make the news. The whole galaxy is focused on the hurricane," the king said. "We're going to have to do a manual search. Screen, show me a live feed of Noun Town."

When nothing appeared to be out of order there, the king asked for a live video feed of Verb Village. Luke noticed something unusual. "Father, why do some of those verbs have wheels?"

"Oh, those are the transitive verbs. They transport action to objects. Do you see the verb *read* there in the sentence, *I read books*?" Luke nodded. *Read* is transitive because it transports its action to books."

"Ohh. So they— action verbs," Luke said.

"Right, but they— more than that. They act on something. So in the sentence, *I read, read*— not a transitive verb. There— no object for

100

the word *read* to act on," the king explained.

"I think I understand," Luke said. "So there— either action verbs with no object or action verbs with objects. The ones with objects have wheels. They're called transport verbs. Right?"

"Very close. They're called transitive verbs. And there is another kind of verb."

Luke nearly interrupted. "Right! The helping verb."

"Correct! But that wasn't the kind of verb I was talking about. I meant linking verbs. They don't have wheels."

"What do they do then?" Luke asked.

"Let's see if we can find some so I can explain. Screen, can you pan around the outskirts of Verb Village. We want to see some linking verbs." The screen panned from side to side. Then it zoomed out.

"There! —that one?" Luke asked. A word could be seen running in the distance.

"That couldn't be a linking verb. They don't run," the king said.

"Your Majesty," Screen interjected. "I do believe Luke is right. The word I'm seeing is, in fact, a linking verb."

"What?" the king exclaimed. "Zoom in on it for me." The word *am* became clearly visible. It was running and leaping joyfully with a chain hanging from each leg.

"It has chains?" Luke asked. "Did the Gremlin put chains on it?"

"No," the king said. "It's supposed to be chained." When Luke gasped, he explained. "Linking verbs are chained to their subject and the word that renames or describes it. For example, I—. I—. Oh, good grammar! I can't say it. Let me see. A linking verb connects the words *I* and *hungry*, for example. Or *I* and *king*."

"I see," Luke said, thinking. "But don't you think linking verbs are unhappy being chained up all the time? That word sure seems happy being set free," Luke said, pointing to the screen.

"Yes, isn't it like slavery?" Ellen added.

"No, it isn't. It's their job."

"Do you pay them?" Kirk asked.

"No, of course, I don't pay them," the king said, getting frustrated. "Listen, this— what linking verbs *do*. They have a wonderful life in Verb Village. Unless they are linked to other words in a sentence, they have no purpose. Sure, that word—happy now. But wait until it gets lonely. And consider what will happen to the English language without linking verbs!"

The queen and the three children thought for a moment and

101

agreed with the king. "Now what do we do?" Kirk asked.

"We're going to need the guardians' help to find the linking verbs," the king said. He requested the guidebook and read the entry on linking verbs to them.

Linking Verbs
Linking verbs connect nouns or pronouns to a descriptive word (adjective) or explanatory noun. The most common linking verbs are forms of the verb **to be** (am, is, are, was, were). *Become* and *seem* are always linking verbs. The verbs *taste, smell, look, sound, feel,* and *appear* can also be linking verbs. The words connected by the linking verb are underlined in the examples below: I *am* the queen. They *seem* sad. It *feels* awful.

"The guardians can help you identify the missing linking verbs. Send out a mission to them ASAP. But then I'd like the three of you to go to Verb Village to find them," the king said. He thought the trip would be good for them.

What does *catastrophic* mean?

What is a transitive verb?

How is a linking verb different?

Chapter 20

"Where's Ellen?" the queen asked one morning.

"I don't know," Luke said. "Have you seen her, Kirk?"

"No, I haven't," Kirk said. "Maybe she is sleeping in."

"I'm going to go check on her," the queen said.

When the queen arrived at Ellen's bedchamber, she found her still in bed. But she was awake. "Ellen, what's wrong? Are you ill?"

"Yes, Mother. I am just so tired." The queen felt Ellen's forehead and it did feel warm.

"I'm going to call the nurse," the queen said.

The nurse agreed that Ellen had a fever. "Are you hungry?" the nurse asked.

"No," Ellen said, shaking her head.

The queen looked at the nurse with concern. "What do you think is wrong with her?"

"I don't know," the nurse said. "It's probably just a cold."

"Let's let her sleep and see how she is later," the queen said. The nurse agreed that this was a good idea. The queen kissed Ellen's forehead and closed the door behind her.

That afternoon the queen went back to check on Ellen. She was quite alarmed by what she saw. Ellen was awake but covered in spots.

"What are they?" Ellen shrieked. "They itch."

"Oh, dear," the queen said. "I think I know, but I better call the doctor."

For the second time that day, a health professional examined Ellen. When he was finished, he turned to the queen and said, "You are right. She has them."

"I have what?" Ellen asked.

"I think we need to call your father," the queen said.

The king arrived, looking concerned. Even though the doctor had confirmed the diagnosis, the king wanted to see for himself. He just could not believe that one of his children had this **dreaded** disease. He thought he had done enough, but alas! His own daughter was suffering from it.

"Don't blame yourself, dear," the queen said. "It happens!"

"Not to my daughter!" the king said **gravely**.

"What do we do now?" the queen asked.

"Tell me what's wrong with me!" Ellen cried. "Is it serious?"

"Yes, it's serious!" the king said.

"You're scaring her," the queen said.

"I'm sorry," he responded. "I don't mean to frighten you."

"You mean I'll live?" Ellen said.

"Oh, my galaxy, yes!" the queen said. "You're not going to die."

"Well, that's a relief," Ellen said. "Are you going to tell me what's wrong with me now?"

"We need to have your brothers here first," the king answered.

Ellen remained worried. She scratched some of the spots on her arm until the queen stopped her. "You'll cause scarring," the queen warned.

"But it itches so much!" Ellen complained.

"We'll get you some lotion that will help," the queen reassured her.

When Kirk and Luke arrived at Ellen's bedchamber, they were alarmed by their parents' behavior.

"What's wrong with her?" Luke asked.

"It's a serious diagnosis," the king said. "I never thought one of my children would suffer from it."

"Tell us what it is, Father," Kirk said.

The king sighed deeply. "She has the prepositions."

"The prepositions!" Luke yelled. "What's that?"

"Shh," the queen said. "Don't say that too loudly."

"Okay, what is the prepositions?" Luke asked, whispering.

"Should we tell him?" the queen asked. The king nodded.

"The prepositions is a disease that gets in you, on you, by you, beside you, on top of you, and even goes through you."

"What causes it?" Kirk asked.

★ ★ ★ ★ ★ ★ ★ ★ ★ ★
dreaded – *feared*
gravely – *seriously*
★ ★ ★ ★ ★ ★ ★ ★ ★ ★

The King sighed and bowed his head. "That's the worst part. People get the prepositions when they don't know them."

The queen nodded. "Yes, we are **devastated** that Ellen has the prepositions. We don't know how we missed teaching them to her."

★ ★ ★ ★ ★ ★ ★ ★ ★ ★

devastated – *overwhelmed*

★ ★ ★ ★ ★ ★ ★ ★ ★ ★

Luke began scratching his arm. His mother noticed and shrieked, "Luke! Why are you scratching?"

"I don't know. It itches." The queen pulled back Luke's sleeve to reveal multiple red spots on his arm.

"This is a disaster!" the king said.

"You better tell me about prepositions before I break out in spots, too," Kirk said. His parents agreed. The king called for the guidebook to be brought to Ellen's bedchamber.

"We should have taught you the prepositions long ago. Learning the prepositions prevents this disease. The king began to read the entry on prepositions from the guidebook.

Prepositions
Prepositions show the position of something in time or space. Prepositions are combined with other words to form a prepositional phrase. A noun or pronoun, called the object of the preposition, comes at the end of the phrase.   **Common prepositions include:**   aboard, about, above, across, against, along, around, amid, among, after, at, except, for, during, down, behind, below, beneath, beside, between, before, beyond, by, in, from, off, on, over, of, until, unto, upon, underneath, since, up, like, near, past, throughout, through, with, within, without, instead, toward, inside, into, to

When he was finished, Ellen said, "I really wish you had read this to me before I got these itchy spots."

"I know!" The queen cried in anguish.

"What can we do now?" Ellen asked. "Is there any cure?"

"You can treat the symptoms," the queen said. "There is a lotion you can use that will help with the itching."

"But the best treatment is to memorize the prepositions," the king said.

"How do we do that fast? I don't know how long I can take this itching," Luke said.

"There are a couple of ways to memorize prepositions quickly," the queen said. First, you can think of positions. Take this little doll for instance. What is her position with respect to this dollhouse?" The queen put the doll inside the house.

"She is inside the house," Ellen answered.

"Exactly, Ellen," the queen said. "*Inside* is a preposition." She then put the doll below the house and asked Luke where she was. When he responded correctly, the queen said the word *underneath* was also a preposition.

"I think I get it!" Luke exclaimed. "Should my spots go away now?"

"I'm afraid it doesn't work that way," the queen said sadly. "You will have to memorize the prepositions. Not all prepositions are position words. Another way to memorize prepositions is with a song."

"Which song?" Luke asked.

"It's called 'The Preposition Song.' I will teach it to you, but I think it's important for Kirk to include it in a mission. We don't want the rest of the young guardians to get sick, do we?"

All three English children agreed. Kirk worked with his mother on a mission called Prepositions.

What does *dreaded* mean?

Why did Ellen and Luke have itchy spots?

What prepositions relate to where you are in space right now?

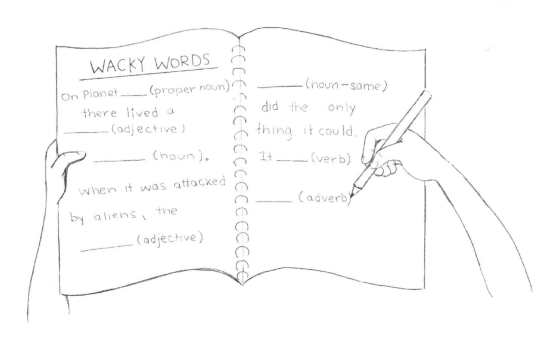

Chapter 21

"We're going to visit Grandma," the queen announced at the breakfast table.

"Are we using the spaceporter?" Luke asked. He hoped they were. He didn't like traveling long distance.

"No. Your father wants to take the carriage."

"But that will take sooo long," Luke whined.

"Luke, we will have lots of time together. And we can see the countryside," the king said.

Luke knew better than to try to change his father's mind. But he wasn't happy about it.

"You could read on the way," the queen said, guessing at what he was thinking.

"Too bumpy," Luke complained.

The king was getting irritated. "We are taking the carriage to visit your grandmother and you're going to enjoy it!"

Luke tried to finish his breakfast without pouting. His siblings saw how Luke's complaints were received and decided to stay silent.

As they were getting into the carriage for their day trip, Ellen remarked on how cold it was.

"Yes, it's refreshing, isn't it?" the king asked.

Ellen nodded weakly but asked for warm blankets. Luke asked if they had plenty of snacks with them. Kirk seemed satisfied to have a camera with him. He hoped to get some shots of the fall **foliage** as they traveled.

★ ★ ★ ★ ★ ★ ★ ★ ★ ★

foliage – *leafage*

reprimanded – *scolded*

chided – *scolded*

★ ★ ★ ★ ★ ★ ★ ★ ★ ★

"Would we be able to stop so I can get better pictures on the way?" he asked. His siblings groaned when his father said they absolutely could. Luke was **reprimanded** when he said that would make the trip take longer than forever.

After they had been traveling for half an hour, the queen had an idea. "Let's play Wacky Words. I'll ask you for a different part of speech and it will become part of a story. Then the story will be funny to read back. Give me a minute."

She took out a notebook and pen from her purse and wrote for several minutes. "Okay, I'm ready. Luke, give me a noun."

"What's a noun again?" Luke asked. His brother and sister groaned. "Sorry! I just need a reminder."

"Luke, nouns live in Noun Town on Person, Place, or Thing Street. Now do you remember?" Kirk asked.

"Oh, yeah," Luke said.

"I think you mean 'oh, yes,' the queen **chided** him.

Luke was embarrassed. "Yes. Okay, let's see. Any noun?" When his mother nodded, he said, "How about Comet?" This was Luke's way of reminding his mother that he was unhappy their dog wasn't coming with them.

"Luke, that's a proper noun because it's a name. I just need a common noun for this Wacky Words story," the queen said.

"All right. How about *sad* then?" Luke said, smirking. "I'm sure Comet is sad that he isn't coming with us."

The queen wrote it down, ignoring Luke's attempt at making her feel guilty. "Okay, Ellen, how about a verb?"

Before Ellen could answer, Luke interrupted. "Sorry, but what's a verb again?" The queen patiently explained that a verb shows action.

Or, as they had recently learned, verbs could link parts of a sentence together.

"Oh, yeah. I mean, oh, yes. Thank you, Mother," Luke said.

"Hm," Ellen began. "How about flower? I love flowers."

"I do, too," the queen said, writing it down. "Now then, I need an adjective, Kirk."

"An adjective," Kirk said, thinking.

"I always get those mixed up with adverbs," Luke said.

"They're easy to keep straight, Luke. Adverbs add to the verb. They tell you how, when, and where," the king explained.

"Right, but adjectives don't add to the jective," Luke said, smirking.

The king laughed. "You have a point. But since an adjective doesn't add to a verb, you know it adds to a noun. It tells you what kind of noun, which noun, or how many of a noun."

"Got it," Luke said. "Hey! Maybe this will help me remember. Adjectives live in Adjective Alley which is adjacent to Noun Town. *Adjacent* means next to. I just learned that."

"What a smart boy I have," the king said.

"I still need an adjective, Kirk," the queen reminded him.

"Okay, how about *flew*?"

"Very well," the queen said, writing it down. "I need another adjective, Luke."

"*Later*," Luke said proudly.

"No, now, Luke," the queen insisted.

"I meant *later* is my adjective," Luke said.

"Oh, sorry," the queen apologized. "I also need a name, so a proper noun. And I need an adverb," the queen said.

Ellen called out the words *freezing* and *twelve*.

The queen wrote them down. "I think I have what I need for this Wacky Words story. I'm ready to read it."

On planet <u>Freezing</u> there lived a <u>flew</u> <u>sad</u>. When it was attacked
       (proper noun)   (adjective) (noun)

by aliens, the <u>later</u> <u>sad</u> did the only thing it could. It <u>flower</u>ed
           (adjective) (same as 1ˢᵗ noun)   (verb)

<u>twelve</u>.
(adverb)

"Pretty funny, don't you think?" the queen asked. The children were slow to respond, which irritated the queen. "I am trying to make

109

this an enjoyable trip for you! I think playing Wacky Words is fun. The least you can do is have good attitudes."

The king was worried she was going to cry. He suspected that his wife was a little tense. She was often nervous about being around his mother. "Dear, you are so clever. And you're an amazing mother, too. Don't you think so, children?" The three English children quickly agreed.

"I thought it was funny. Didn't you think it was funny, dear?" the queen asked. She was obviously hoping he agreed.

"It was very goofy. And that's the point, correct?" He waited for her to nod. "Can you read it again? I think it will be funnier the second time."

The queen read, "On planet Freezing there lived a flew sad. When it was attacked by aliens, the later sad did the only thing it could. It flowered twelve." When she was finished, she looked confused. "Hm. A flew sad. That's strange. It flowered twelve? It's funny strange, not funny ha-ha." Her family readily agreed. "Maybe I'm just terrible at writing Wacky Words," she sighed. "I know! I have a Wacky Words app on my tablet. We can play with that!" Her spirits lifted immediately, so the children were happy to participate.

When she opened the app, a message appeared on the screen. "Wacky Words is having technical difficulties. Our engineers are working hard to fix the problem."

"It appears that we can't play. I'm so disappointed," the queen said. She discussed other travel games they could play.

Kirk used the time to check the news on his communicator. "Father," he said. "We have a problem. There is chaos on planet Sentence. Apparently, there are verbs insisting that they live in Noun Town. There are adverbs in Adjective Alley and the adjectives are quite upset."

"That makes no sense. How could words become confused about where they belong?" the king asked.

"The city signs have been stolen," Kirk said after reading more.

"This is a crisis. Dear, contact my mother and let her know that we will have to reschedule our visit." The king directed the driver to take them back to their castle. The queen finished her conversation with the queen mother. Then the king said, "I just thought of something else that will lift your spirits. You're not bad at Wacky Words. The parts of speech were all mixed up. That's why it wasn't funny." The queen was very much relieved.

When the royal family arrived home, the king ordered that new signs be created for the cities on planet Sentence. "But I need the guardians' help," he told the children. "Send out a mission called Parts of Speech. We need to get all the words back where they belong or not being able to play Wacky Words will be the least of our worries."

What does *chided* mean?

Is the word *flower* a verb? If not, what part of speech is it?

Why wasn't the Wacky Words story very funny?

Chapter 22

Luke couldn't wait. His whole family was visiting the Grammar Rocks. But even better, many of his friends were going, too. His father had agreed to lead a field trip for his Grammar Guys troop.

He could see that his father was more stressed than usual. The king wanted to make sure they had the appropriate safety supplies — a first-aid kit, a good map, and plenty of water. It was a hot day and another troop had gotten stranded on the Grammar Rocks trails without enough water. Luke didn't know how they would be able to carry all the water his father wanted to bring.

His mother was more concerned with snacks. "Boys need food," she was saying to the kitchen staff. In this case, Luke had to agree with his mother. The Grammar Guys could eat a lot – especially the older boys.

Luke focused on filling his pack. He was taking binoculars, his own map, a notebook, and a pen. When they arrived at the trail, they would be given water, snacks, and a list of words to find on the trail. Luke hoped to find most of them. At the end of the trip, the boys would compare lists.

He couldn't wait for the other boys to arrive at the castle. His father had arranged for a large spacecopter to take the group to the mountain. The king was counting on plenty of other fathers to help chaperone the group.

When several of the dads who were leaders canceled, the king became very anxious. The queen tried to calm him. "Dear, you have all the supplies you need. And these are good boys. You'll be fine."

"I hope so," the king said, sounding unconvinced.

When the group arrived at the trailhead, the king took out his clipboard. He called out everyone's names and checked them off as they answered. The king asked two adult leaders to each go with a smaller group of boys. He wrote down which trail they planned to take. He gave everyone a pep talk before they left. "Remember: safety first! Stay together, okay? Make sure your leader knows where you are." The boys nodded. When he asked for the twentieth time if they had enough water, they groaned and promised him they did.

Luke and his closest friends were going with the king. Though his father was worrying for nothing, Luke was proud to be with him. He hoped his father would relax and have fun.

The boys spotted some words on their lists immediately. They were carved into the rocks and were easy to see. That energized the boys and they started walking faster. "Wait up!" the king said, panting. "I need to work out more," he muttered to himself.

The king looked up at the sky and noticed it was considerably darker than when they had arrived. He checked the forecast on his communicator. No rain in the forecast. That was a relief. He hiked quickly, trying to catch up to the boys. By the time he did, it had started to rain. "No," he groaned. "Why are weather forecasts always wrong?"

"Maybe it will be a short shower," Luke suggested.

"Maybe," the king agreed. But as soon as he'd said it, the rain started falling faster and heavier.

"Don't worry. It feels good," Luke said. "And we definitely won't run out of water," he joked.

"Indeed," the king said, laughing. He stopped laughing when he heard thunder. "Uh-oh. We can't be out here when there's lightning. We have to find cover." He took out his map and showed Luke a cave that was back the way they'd come. "I need to contact the leaders and tell them to bring the boys there."

The king tried to use his communicator to contact the troop leaders, but it wouldn't connect. "I can't get a signal," he said, just as lightning lit up the darkened sky. "Boys! We have to get to the cave!" he yelled. He was ready to direct them back down the trail when he realized they weren't all there. He started to panic when the remaining boys said they didn't know where the others had gone. He was responsible for them and if something happened to them, he would feel horrible.

The wind picked up as he tried to decide what to do "— go look for them!" Luke shouted.

The king thought that made sense. He would go look for them while Luke led the other boys to the cave. "— take the boys to the cave!" the king shouted. Luke thought his father would take the boys to the cave while he looked for the missing boys. In the confusion, the two led the boys further up the trail as they called for the missing hikers.

The king finally grabbed Luke. "— have to go back!" he shouted. Luke thought he was going to go back down the trail to the cave.

"— keep looking!" Luke shouted. The king thought Luke told him to keep looking for the boys. Once again, they continued further on the trail together, with the boys following.

The group was soaked and jumped every time lightning struck. They were in a dangerous position and they knew it. "— are not here!" Luke shouted.

"— want to go back!" the king shouted. The two finally understood that they had to go back down the trail. The wind and rain in the darkness made **navigating treacherous**. It felt like it took an **eternity**, but they arrived at the cave. There they found the missing boys from their party.

★ ★ ★ ★ ★ ★ ★ ★ ★ ★

navigating – *proceeding*

treacherous – *dangerous*

eternity – *forever*

★ ★ ★ ★ ★ ★ ★ ★ ★ ★

"— were worried about you," one of the leaders said, hugging the boys. He would have hugged the king, but he didn't think it was appropriate.

"Is — here?" the king asked.

The leader who greeted him was confused at first, but then said, "Oh, — went looking for you."

"For me?" the king was alarmed. Now he was responsible for another leader being in danger. The king was ready to go out looking for him when he entered the cave.

"— was worried," the missing leader said.

"— know. — too!" the king said. He looked at Luke. "—have another problem."

Luke nodded. When the rain finally stopped, the king said, "— should go home. — is too slick on the trail now." The other leaders agreed.

When the soggy group arrived back at the castle, it was the queen's turn to be upset. "— are soaked! — happened?" she shrieked.

"— will tell you, dear. But first, — have to solve a bigger problem." The king quickly changed into dry clothes and had the three children meet him in the library. "— are missing words," he started. The children nodded. They'd noticed.

"Give me news from planet Sentence, please," he told Screen. Nothing appeared in the search results. "Okay, look for anything having to do with subjects," the king said.

"Found this, Your Majesty." It was a commercial for research participants.

"We're looking for subjects," a man in a white lab coat said. "You can make the universe a better place to live by helping us with this important research. But that's not all. You'll be paid very well for participating in this isolation study. Contact us as soon as possible. We're counting on you." An email address flashed on the screen.

"— is an isolation study?" Luke asked.

"— means the subjects won't have access to the outside world anymore," the king explained.

"And can't be part of sentences," Kirk added. Kirk opened the guidebook to the entry on sentence subjects and read.

Subjects
The subject of a sentence is the noun or pronoun that is doing or being. It is usually found at the beginning of a sentence. To find the subject, find the verb and ask, "Who or what?" followed by the verb.
A **simple subject** is only the noun or pronoun the sentence is about.
The complete subject includes the adjectives and article adjectives (a, an, the) that describe the subject. For example:
The five boys were terrified.
The simple subject is *boys*. The complete subject is *The five boys*.

"— have to get the subjects out of the study, right, Father?" Ellen asked.

"Right. — can work on that, but — need the guardians' help. Can — work on that?"

The three young guardians agreed and started work on a mission called Subjects.

What does *treacherous* mean in the story?

Ellen said, "— have to get the subjects out of the study, right, Father?" What word couldn't she say?

Why did the king and Luke keep getting confused on the mountain?

Chapter 23

The king was in a surprisingly cheery mood, considering it was election season. He constantly complained about the negative ads that candidates ran about their opponents. There were so many lies and exaggerations, he said, that the people didn't want to vote for anyone.

He explained his good mood with the paper. "Look at this! Parliament has passed a law that will eliminate the nasty election ads. There will be no more **slander**. We can just hear about the issues."

★ ★ ★ ★ ★ ★ ★ ★ ★ ★

slander – *insults*

★ ★ ★ ★ ★ ★ ★ ★ ★ ★

The whole family expressed appreciation for the law. They were happy because the king was happy.

"Will this apply to students, too? We are having a mock election as part of our government studies. Will this require the posters we make to be positive?" Kirk asked.

"Absolutely!" the king said. "Are you doing a debate for your election, Kirk?" The king was pleased when Kirk said they were. "It's an excellent opportunity for you to learn about our electoral process. And you won't have all the slander that we've had in the past. Now if we could just pass a law that kept the ads on television from being louder than other programs. I hate that!"

A few weeks later, the first televised debate was set to be aired. The king insisted the entire family watch. That way they would know the issues affecting their planet. "I am sure they will discuss taxes, the environment, and the safety of our galaxy," the king said.

Luke tried not to irritate his father by showing his boredom. "How long will the debate last?" he asked.

"About two hours."

"Two hours?" Luke repeated in horror. Then he corrected himself. "Okay. Two hours." He tried to think of something else he could do while it was on that wouldn't get him into trouble.

The queen noticed Luke's attitude. "Perhaps we could have popcorn while we watch?" she asked. Luke was very enthusiastic about the idea and went with the queen to the kitchen.

"Do you have a favorite candidate, Father?" Kirk asked.

"Not yet. I want to hear what they have to say first."

When the debate started, the moderators introduced themselves. Then the candidates briefly introduced themselves. The first question was, "What is your position on the planet's tax rate?"

A tall, smiling man had the opportunity to answer first. "Well, I —," he began. The man to his right interrupted him. The moderator told the interrupting candidate to let the first one answer. "Okay, I —" he started again when he was interrupted by a third candidate.

"Hm. I guess they didn't pass an interrupting law, right, Father?" Kirk chuckled.

The king didn't seem to think it was very funny. "Let him answer the question!" he yelled at the screen.

The moderator once again asked that the first candidate be given a chance to speak. "I —," he started. He took a deep breath. "Yes, I —"

"He must be nervous," Kirk thought out loud.

"We —" the candidate began. When he didn't continue, he was interrupted by several other candidates.

"This is ridiculous!" the king complained. "Start discussing the issues!"

"Perhaps this topic isn't the best one to start with," the moderator said. "Let's discuss the environment. What, if any, policy change do you think our planet should make to protect the environment?" he asked. "Let's begin on this end of the stage this time," he said, pointing to his left.

A calm-looking woman started to answer. "Okay, I —, we —." She looked **confounded** when she had no more words.

★ ★ ★ ★ ★ ★ ★ ★ ★ ★

confounded – *confused*

★ ★ ★ ★ ★ ★ ★ ★ ★ ★

"Wow! She's nervous, too," Kirk said.

"We'll come back to you," the moderator said compassionately. He gave the woman to her left an opportunity to speak.

"Yes, I —, I —," she started. She shook her head in disbelief.

"No one has said anything and the debate has been going on for twenty minutes now," the king roared.

The moderator looked alarmed. He knew that they would be losing viewers. He whispered to the woman moderator to his left. She started to speak. "The next question —. Next, we —. I —." She patted the arm of the moderator to her left and quickly made her way out of the auditorium.

"Is everyone ill?" the king asked.

"Could it be food poisoning?" Ellen suggested. She was suddenly finding the whole debate very interesting.

The debate broadcast broke for a commercial just as Luke and the queen returned with popcorn.

The king started to explain to them what had been happening. "The debate —. The candidates —. The moderators —." His eyes grew wide as he realized he was speaking like the people at the debate. "The Gremlin," he said resignedly.

"Oh, no!" the queen cried.

"Screen," the king said. "Planet Sentence. New law?" Screen responded by searching for news on recently enacted laws there. The king touched one story on the screen that mentioned the new election law. He read the story silently. A judge had put all words that could be used to attack candidates under a **gag order**. The words would not be allowed to be used.

★ ★ ★ ★ ★ ★ ★ ★ ★ ★

gag order – *ban*

★ ★ ★ ★ ★ ★ ★ ★ ★ ★

The story included a picture of groups of words behind a taped-off area that said, "Quarantine." The unusual move of isolating words was being taken for the public's protection, the article said. The order was to be enforced during the entire election season. The king motioned for his family to read the article as well.

"What a mess!" Kirk declared.

The king nodded. "All words that say anything about someone else," the king explained. He called his butler and said, "Guidebook." When it was brought to him, he opened the book to the entry called Predicates. He had each of them read it to themselves.

Predicates

A predicate is the part of the sentence that says what the subject does or is. The **complete predicate** includes the verb, adverbs, and everything besides the subject. The **simple predicate** is the verb or verb phrase. In the sentence, "The little girl played with her dolls," *played with her dolls* is the complete predicate and *played* is the simple predicate. To find the predicate, ask, "What is being said about?" after the subject.

"You —," the king said, looking at his children.

"Mission?" Ellen asked. The king nodded again.

The three children began working on a mission called "Predicates." In the meantime, their father hoped to have the gag order lifted.

What does *slander* mean?

What is a predicate?

Why couldn't the candidates answer the questions?

Chapter 24

"You won't believe who just called," the king announced. It was Saturday morning and the three English children were suddenly wide awake.

"Who? Who?" they asked in a chorus.

"The producers of *Wild Galaxy*," the king said proudly.

"No way! Awesome!" the kids exclaimed.

"Yes way," the king said. "He wants one of you to star on an episode."

Kirk, Luke, and Ellen were thrilled. The queen, however, was upset. "You can't be serious! That show is too dangerous for young children. It's so terrifying I can't watch as it is."

"Oh, dear, this is a once-in-a-lifetime opportunity. I would love to do it. But the producer wants one of the children. He thinks viewers will love it."

"I'm sure many people would love to see one of my children in mortal danger," the queen said. Her lips trembled and her eyes welled up with tears.

"No one has ever died on the show, Mother," Kirk said.

"Not yet," the queen **retorted**.

★ ★ ★ ★ ★ ★ ★ ★ ★ ★

retorted – *snapped*

★ ★ ★ ★ ★ ★ ★ ★ ★ ★

"Wait! Did the producer say what the adventure was?" Luke asked.

"He wants you to choose. One of you will either snowmobile at the South Pole, trek through the Grammarhara Desert, or climb Mt. Grammarest."

"You must be joking! He wants a child to do one of those risky things? For ratings?" the queen objected.

The king sighed. "I really think it's perfectly safe. They will have an expert with our son or daughter the whole time."

"Please, Mother? YOLO," Ellen pleaded.

"YOLO? Is that another of those acronyms?"

"Yes. It means you only live once," Kirk explained.

"That's my point exactly!" the queen cried. "Why risk your one and only life?"

The king ignored his wife's complaint. He said, "We have to decide which of you will go on the adventure. It's not an easy choice, I know. I wish you could all go. What are your thoughts?"

"Well," Ellen started, "Kirk and I could snowmobile and climb."

"Yes," the king said. "You could. But that isn't a decision. Kirk, what do you think?"

"Well, Ellen and I could climb and trek," he answered.

The king looked **baffled**. "So you don't want to make a decision, either. Luke, what about you? Want to make a case for being on the show?"

★ ★ ★ ★ ★ ★ ★ ★ ★ ★

baffled – *confused*

diplomatic – *polite*

★ ★ ★ ★ ★ ★ ★ ★ ★ ★

"Kirk and I could trek and snowmobile," Luke answered cautiously.

"I suppose I should be annoyed. But I think you're trying to be **diplomatic**. I'm proud of that. Dear," he said, turning to the queen, "you and I are going to have to discuss and decide this."

The queen nodded and the couple went to the bedchamber to talk. "I know you don't want any of them to go, but who should go, in your opinion?"

"Kirk and Ellen could snowmobile and climb," the queen said.

"Yes, they're the oldest. But let's not worry about which adventure yet. Of Kirk and Ellen, who should go?" the king pressed her.

"Kirk and Luke could trek and snowmobile."

"Is this your way of keeping them from going?" The king could no longer hide his frustration. The queen looked like she was going to start crying. Before the king could apologize, his steward knocked on the door.

"Sire," he said breathlessly when admitted to the room. "There is a situation."

The king went with him to his study where he was briefed by the director of the GBI (Galactic Bureau of Investigation). "There's a remote area on planet Sentence called Wordo. There are subjects and predicates in a compound there. They are in a standoff with our agents. We believe they are armed and dangerous. We want your permission to destroy the compound," the director said.

"What? No! Do we even know which subjects and predicates are in the compound?"

"No, Your Highness. We don't."

"Okay. How do you know they're dangerous?"

"We got an anonymous tip."

The king sighed. "Don't you see that this is probably the Gremlin's doing? We can't destroy subjects and predicates, even a small number of them. It would be disastrous."

"But they refuse to leave the compound."

"Are they able to? Is it possible they're locked inside?"

The director looked thoughtful. "We haven't determined that. We were afraid of being fired upon."

"Well, can you find out?"

"Yes, Your Highness." The director left in a rush.

The king returned to his bedchamber. "I know why you won't make a decision on *Wild Galaxy*."

"You do?" the queen said hopefully. "So you're not going to let them go on the show?"

"That's not what I meant." The king explained the situation in Wordo. The subjects and predicates had created compound subjects and predicates. "You kept using multiple subjects and predicates, and so did the kids."

The king had the children brought to his bedchamber. He had already had the guidebook brought to him.

The king explained what was happening for the second time. Then he read the entry on compound subjects and predicates.

Compound Subjects and Predicates

A compound subject is more than one subject with the same predicate.
The <u>boys</u> and <u>girls</u> play board games.
A compound predicate is two or more verbs with the same subject.
The boys <u>played</u> board games and <u>jumped</u> on the trampoline.
Compound subjects and predicates are combined by coordinating conjunctions (e.g., *and, or*).

When the king finished reading, the GBI director contacted him on his communicator. "Your Highness, you were right about the compound. They were locked in. But we still can't get them out. Do you think the guardians could help?"

The three children overhead the director and were already saying yes. The king promised they would join the GBI before he ended the call.

"But is it safe?" the queen worried aloud.

"Definitely. It will be an adventure for them," the king reassured her.

"Speaking of adventure, will Kirk and I trek and snowmobile?" Luke asked.

"We'll decide that when you get back," the king answered.

"I have an idea for getting the subjects and predicates out," Kirk said. "But we'll need to send out a mission."

The three guardians finished a mission called Compound Subjects and Predicates. Then they left for planet Sentence.

What does *diplomatic* mean?

What is a compound subject?

Why didn't the queen or children give only one answer to the king's question?

WOMAN'S UNIVERSE

Grammar Queen loves cooking pets and decorating

Chapter 25

The queen squealed from the sunroom, getting Ellen's attention. "What is it, Mother?" she asked.

The queen was giddy and held up a copy of *Woman's Universe* that she had just received in the mail. "I'm on the cover!" she gushed. She cradled it to her chest. "I just can't believe it."

"Was this for that photo shoot they did here at the castle?" Ellen asked.

"Yes! They took pictures of me cooking. They wanted to see the redecorating I've been doing and our new saltwater aquarium. That reminds me. Cook will be so excited to see this, too. Let's go show her."

Cook was indeed excited to see the magazine cover and to see the queen so happy.

"I'm so grateful to you, Cook," the queen said. "If you hadn't given me cooking lessons, I doubt *Woman's Universe* would have put me on the cover." When Cook **demurred**, the queen insisted. "Before my cooking hobby, I wasn't really doing anything."

★ ★ ★ ★ ★ ★ ★ ★ ★ ★

demurred – *objected*

★ ★ ★ ★ ★ ★ ★ ★ ★ ★

"She wasn't," Ellen agreed, and the three of them laughed.

At dinner that evening, the queen couldn't stop talking about the magazine. "I've read the article and they did such a lovely job. I don't think it was exaggerated, and it wasn't mean, either," she said.

"That's lovely, dear. Maybe you'll inspire more women to take up cooking as a hobby," the king said.

"I hadn't even thought of that," the queen said, grinning.

"Maybe they'll want you to have your own cooking show!" Ellen suggested.

"Now we may be getting a little ahead of ourselves," the queen said, but it was obvious she liked the idea. Ellen did give the queen an idea, though. "We should watch *Galaxy Gourmet* for our family time tonight! Cook," she called loudly. "Will you watch *Galaxy Gourmet* with us? Maybe we could co-host our own cooking show one day!"

Cook came through the kitchen doors blushing. "Your Highness, I would love to! Let me get my cleaning chores finished and I'll join you. In the media room?" When the queen agreed, Cook returned to the kitchen humming happily. Momentarily, the family heard her telling the staff to hurry.

"Uh, I have a paper I'm working on. Would it be all right if I didn't watch the show with you?" Kirk asked.

"Oh. Well, your education comes first. Of course, you may be excused, Kirk," the queen answered.

"Hey! That reminds me. I have to finish a book for literature class. Sorry, I won't be able to watch with you," Luke said in a way that suggested he wasn't sad.

"You, too? All right. I want you to read," the queen said. "It looks like it will be the four of us then. You," she said, looking at the king, "me, Ellen, and Cook."

"Actually..." the king started hesitantly. "I was planning on writing more stories. I don't want to disappoint you, though."

The queen sighed. "It's okay. I know you don't care for these shows anyway." The king tried to hide his relief.

After dinner was finished, the three ladies sat down to watch their favorite cooking show. The queen wanted to watch with her own future show in mind. The evening news was just finishing up. A male news anchor said, "Now for a story that everyone is talking about, concerning our own queen." The queen gasped as a female reporter took the story over.

"People can't stop talking about this magazine cover, featuring the queen. She looks beautiful in her castle kitchen," she said. "But that's not what has created all the buzz. Pay close attention to the title: Queen enjoys cooking pets and decorating. People have been discussing what kind of pets the queen might enjoy cooking. Some have mentioned that it's been a long time since they've seen Comet, the royal family's dog. Could the family have eaten him?"

Video footage of a group of protesters outside the castle played while the reporter continued. "Animal rights activists are demanding that the queen stop cooking pets immediately."

The queen covered her mouth in horror. "Are they out there now?" She called for the butler to check for them while Cook and Ellen tried to comfort her.

"Don't take it so hard, Your Majesty," Cook said. "I know you've never cooked a pet in your life. This is all a misunderstanding."

"But how can I prove it? Those people believe what they've read," the queen said **forlornly**.

★ ★ ★ ★ ★ ★ ★ ★ ★ ★

forlornly – *sadly*

★ ★ ★ ★ ★ ★ ★ ★ ★ ★

"I'm going to go get Father," Ellen declared. The queen didn't object. Ellen knew they had a serious problem.

When the king joined the ladies in the media room, he asked to see the magazine. When the queen retrieved it for him, he frowned. "I see why they think you enjoy cooking pets."

"You do?" the queen asked.

"Yes! The magazine editor left off a comma. Look here. There should be a comma after the word *cooking*."

The queen fumed. "Do you think they did this on purpose? And to think I thought they were honoring me!"

"I doubt they did it on purpose, dear," the king said. "I need to check something."

He left and returned with the newspaper. "It looks like the magazine isn't the only thing affected by a lack of commas. Read this headline."

"Very Pretty King," the queen read. She giggled.

"Yes, very funny. There is supposed to be a comma before king. But this article about the city garden I had planted makes it look like they're calling me pretty," the king explained.

"Wish they had called me pretty instead of suggesting that I cook pets," the queen said. "Why are commas missing?"

"That's what I have to find out," the king said. He ordered Screen to give him an update from planet Sentence. "It's just as I feared," he said a few minutes later. "It's the latest result of the war over comma usage. Look at the comma signs in a pile." He pointed to a photo on the screen.

"I didn't know commas were important enough to fight over," Ellen said.

"Oh, indeed they are. The articles about your mother and me are just the beginning of the confusion that will result," the king said. "I need to talk with your brothers."

The king requested the guidebook from the library. When Kirk and Luke arrived, he turned to the entry on commas. "There are a number of comma rules you need to know. But I want to share two of them with you today."

Commas

A comma is a punctuation mark (,) that is used to show a pause between sentence parts. Proper usage can prevent confusion. There are a number of rules for the correct use of commas.

First, commas are used to separate words in a list of three or more items.
The children love reading, writing, and playing games.
Use of a comma before the word *and* at the end of a list is known as the Oxford comma. If you use it in your writing, you should use it **consistently**.

A second rule for comma usage is to separate the name of the person you are speaking to with commas. Note the difference in meanings below:
I will call you, Angel. (The person is going to call someone who is named Angel.)
I will call you Angel. (The person is giving someone the name Angel.)

"I didn't know commas were so important," Kirk said.

"I didn't, either!" The queen said. "I do now."

"What are we going to do about the commas?" Luke asked.

"First, I have to get all of the commas on planet Sentence put back in place. Obviously, I can't do it alone."

"Do you need us to go to planet Sentence?" Kirk asked.

When the king agreed, Luke asked, "We are going to need the guardians' help too, right?"

"Indeed," the king answered.

"But how will I convince people that I don't cook pets?" the queen worried aloud.

"I have an idea," Ellen said.

The three English children worked together to create a mission they called Commas.

★ ★ ★ ★ ★ ★ ★ ★ ★ ★
consistently – *always*
★ ★ ★ ★ ★ ★ ★ ★ ★ ★

What does *consistently* mean?

Why did people think the queen enjoyed cooking pets?

Where should the comma go in the headline "Very Pretty King"?

Unit IV: Adventures in Composition & Speaking

Chapter 26

"We need to talk with you, children," the king announced one evening. "We feel you could benefit from some tutoring."

"Tutoring? Why? We've been doing well in our studies, haven't we?" Kirk asked.

"Yes, you've been doing fine. But we feel you could excel as writers under the **tutelage** of a master."

★ ★ ★ ★ ★ ★ ★ ★ ★

tutelage – *instruction*

extravagant – *excessive*

★ ★ ★ ★ ★ ★ ★ ★ ★

"A master? Cool," Luke murmured.

"Yes, very cool, Luke. Would you like to hear whom we have employed to teach you?" the king asked.

When the children nodded enthusiastically, the queen told them. "It's Mr. Wordagi, the famous author." She seemed excited enough to burst.

"No way!" Luke exclaimed. "Who's that?"

The rest of the family laughed. "He has written several award-winning children's titles, Luke. He is one of the most respected authors of our time," the king explained.

"Wow. And he's going to teach us?" Luke asked.

"Yes," the queen said. "We felt it wasn't **extravagant** to hire him because the three of you teach the rest of the guardians."

"That makes sense," Kirk said. "I'm looking forward to meeting him."

"When will he come?" Ellen asked.

"Tomorrow," the king said.

When Kirk had time, he asked Screen to do some research on Mr. Wordagi. He learned that he refused interviews, preferring to spend his time writing. Kirk was surprised that he wanted to teach three kids if that was his style.

The next morning Mr. Wordagi arrived. Kirk wasn't particularly surprised that he wasn't a smiler. He wasn't smiling in any of the photos he had seen. But that did make him nervous. It could be hard to sit through sessions with a teacher who wasn't very social.

Luke leaped forward to shake Mr. Wordagi's hand vigorously. He was obviously surprised when Mr. Wordagi gave him a lukewarm reception. Ellen curtsied graciously and said hello. Mr. Wordagi didn't smile.

"Where will we be working?" Mr. Wordagi asked the king.

"I planned to have you in the studio. It has a lot of natural light and—," the king started to explain.

Mr. Wordagi cut him off. "Very well. Please show me to the room."

★ ★ ★ ★ ★ ★ ★ ★ ★ ★

demeanor – *manner*

★ ★ ★ ★ ★ ★ ★ ★ ★ ★

The king seemed just as surprised by his **demeanor** as Luke had been. "Certainly," he said, trying not to show his annoyance.

When they arrived at the studio, the king said, "Please let us know if you need anything while you are here."

"Yes," Mr. Wordagi said. "I will." Then he motioned as if to dismiss the king.

The English children were horrified and waited to see how their father would respond. The king's face reddened and he seemed about to speak but thought better of it. He left without saying a word.

Kirk hoped Mr. Wordagi was such a great teacher that it was worth his father being irritated.

"Now then," Mr. Wordagi said. "Do you have paper and a writing instrument?"

Kirk, Luke, and Ellen nodded.

"Very well. And the Screen in this room is fully functional? Yes?"

"Yes," Kirk agreed.

Mr. Wordagi asked Screen to produce a file he had prepared in advance. When it was displayed, he explained, "This is a paragraph from the book, *The Adventures of Pinocchio*. You will copy it. Copy every word; copy every punctuation mark. Do you understand?"

They nodded and looked to him for more instruction. "Get started!" he ordered them.

The three children nervously began copying the words into their notebooks. As Kirk worked, he glanced up at Mr. Wordagi. He was also writing in a notebook. Kirk wondered if he was working on his next book.

Kirk finished his copying first, then Ellen, and finally Luke. They looked at Mr. Wordagi expectantly. When he finally looked up at them, he asked, "What is it?"

The children squirmed in their seats. "Sir, we are finished copying the paragraph," Kirk explained nervously.

"Once?" he asked.

"Yes."

"Do it again," he ordered sternly.

"The same paragraph?" Kirk asked.

Mr. Wordagi seemed irritated by the question. "Copy it until I tell you to stop."

Kirk glanced at Luke and Ellen. Their eyes communicated their horror at the assignment. When they hesitated, Mr. Wordagi commanded, "Begin!" The three of them quickly returned to writing.

It seemed as though hours had passed when Mr. Wordagi told them they could stop copying the paragraph. Their writing hands ached and they slumped over the table they were sitting at.

"You will come back to this room tomorrow, ready to write," Mr. Wordagi stated as a fact.

"Are you going to teach us how to write then?" Luke asked, massaging his writing hand.

Mr. Wordagi left the room wordlessly, leaving the children astonished. "Is Father punishing us for something we don't remember doing?" Luke asked.

"Maybe he is nervous and doesn't know what to teach us. He is afraid of disappointing Mother and Father," Ellen suggested.

"From what I've read, he isn't very social," Kirk explained.

"Whatever he's being paid is a waste," Luke declared. "Except I think my handwriting speed is improving," he said, grinning.

"Let's get out of here. I'm starving!" Ellen declared.

The three English children didn't have to discuss whether to tell their parents or not. They just didn't say anything. They knew their parents had paid a lot of money and were very excited about Mr. Wordagi. So their answers to questions about him were vague.

"We definitely worked hard!" Luke said, smiling. His parents nodded with satisfaction.

The next day, the children were hopeful for a real writing lesson. Mr. Wordagi was already in the studio, writing something in his notebook. "Now then. You'll see we are doing something new today. On the screen is a paragraph from *The Secret Garden*. Copy it. Begin now."

Ellen's eyes grew wide as she realized that her writing hand was in for the same treatment as yesterday. Luke felt like crying. Kirk was worried, but he copied the paragraph as instructed.

When Mr. Wordagi dismissed them for the day, Kirk told Luke and Ellen what he was thinking. "He has to be working for the Gremlin."

Kirk's two younger siblings agreed. "So what do we do? We have to get him fired," Ellen said. Luke nodded.

"We'll have to tell Father even though he'll be upset," Kirk concluded.

At dinner that evening, the queen began asking about their writing lesson. Kirk explained what had been happening. "He puts up a paragraph from a book and has us copy it."

"The whole time!" Luke complained.

"He isn't teaching us to write at all!" Ellen added.

The children were surprised at the king's expression. He seemed amused. "What books were the paragraphs from?" the king asked.

"*The Adventures of Pinocchio* and *The Secret Garden*," Kirk answered.

"Believe me, I won't forget those titles!" Luke exclaimed.

"Those are classic books, of course," the king said.

"Right, but he hasn't taught us anything about writing," Kirk said. "We are pretty sure he is working with the Gremlin."

The king laughed heartily. "My dear children, Mr. Wordagi is not working with the Gremlin."

"How can you be so sure?" Kirk asked.

"Because he is asking you to do something that will help you become great writers. The Gremlin would never do that."

"Copying paragraphs will help us become great writers?" Luke asked. He was confused.

"Yes," the king said, calling the butler. He asked him to have the guidebook brought to him. When it arrived, he turned to the article on copywork and read.

Copywork
Copywork is writing pieces of excellent literature or nonfiction by hand. Copywork teaches literature, vocabulary, spelling, grammar, punctuation, memorization, composition, and penmanship. Imitating a master's style with copywork is a very effective way of learning to write well.

"So all this copying we've been doing is a good thing?" Luke looked horrified.

The queen laughed. "Yes, Luke. I not only learned to write this way, but I memorized my math facts, too. I copied them until I had mastered them."

"Your mother is right. Copywork is the fastest way to become an excellent writer. You can memorize historical facts and inspiring quotes with copywork, too," the king said.

"So you're not going to fire Mr. Wordagi?" Luke asked, disappointment obvious in his tone.

The king tried not to laugh, but couldn't help it. "No, Luke. You will keep working with Mr. Wordagi. But, he will only be here three days a week."

"That's a relief!" Ellen said, laughing. The rest of the family laughed, too.

"So copywork really can make me a good writer?" Kirk asked.

"Definitely, son. I learned more from copying the masters' work than anything else," the king replied. When Kirk looked thoughtful, the king asked what he was considering.

"I know Mr. Wordagi can't teach everyone and wouldn't want to," Kirk said, smirking. "But I'm thinking that the guardians should do copywork, too. We need to be good writers to protect the galaxy."

"Kirk, I'm so proud of you. I agree wholeheartedly," the king said.

Luke and Ellen worked with Kirk to send out a mission called Copywork right away.

What does *extravagant* mean?

Why did the children think Mr. Wordagi was working with the Gremlin?

What does copywork teach?

Chapter 27

"I did it!" Kirk shrieked. He was unusually excited as he came into the sunroom.

"What did you do?" the queen asked. She looked up from her tablet.

"I programmed my robot to talk," Kirk said proudly.

"That's wonderful! Let's see," the queen said. His siblings agreed so loudly that it got the king's attention, too.

Kirk left and quickly returned with a small robot holding a tray. Kirk said, "Servant mode" and the robot came to life. It moved toward the queen.

"I bring drinks," it said.

The queen applauded enthusiastically. "Kirk, I'm so proud of you!" she said.

The king was just about to ask what else it could say when it moved toward him and said, "I bring snacks."

"Kirk, that's excellent, son," the king said, beaming. "The only thing it needs is real drinks and snacks."

Kirk agreed and ran to the kitchen to get some for his robot to deliver. He returned with Cook in tow. She shook her head and pronounced Kirk amazing. Kirk put a couple of drinks with lids and snacks on the tray. Luke insisted on having the first drink delivered to him. Kirk told Luke the command to get the robot to come to him. He was thrilled when it obeyed him.

Next, the king repeated the command and was able to have a snack delivered. "I love it," he declared, eating the treat he took from the tray.

"I'm not sure snacks on demand is a good idea for you," the queen warned. "At least Cook will make you feel guilty when you **overindulge**."

★ ★ ★ ★ ★ ★ ★ ★ ★ ★

overindulge – *overeat*

★ ★ ★ ★ ★ ★ ★ ★ ★ ★

The robot repeated, "I bring snacks," and everyone laughed.

"Can you program it to clean my room?" Luke asked.

"Mine, too?" Ellen agreed.

"For sure!" Kirk said. He left with the robot, saying he had a lot of programming to do.

"I'm going to finish my paper. I'm going to work out," the king said.

"I'm going to read. I'm going to look at decorating photos," the queen said.

"I'm going to read. I'm going to help Cook first," Ellen said, walking out of the room.

Luke laughed. "You all sound like Kirk's robot." When his parents ignored him, Luke decided to go see what Kirk was doing.

Luke found Kirk already busy at his computer. "Are you going to program it to clean my room first?" Luke asked.

"I'm going to program it to clean your room. I'm going to program it to clean Ellen's room," Kirk said.

"Why is everyone talking like that?" Luke asked.

"Like what?" Kirk answered with a question.

"Like your robot," Luke said.

"You will have to be quiet to stay. You will have to go," Kirk **admonished** him.

★ ★ ★ ★ ★ ★ ★ ★ ★ ★

admonished – *scolded*

★ ★ ★ ★ ★ ★ ★ ★ ★ ★

"Wait. I can stay if I'm quiet, or do I have to go?" Luke asked.

"You will have to be quiet to stay. You will have to go," Kirk repeated, getting irritated.

"Okay. You're acting weird, so I'm going to go," Luke said. He decided to see what Ellen and Cook were up to in the kitchen. It was close to lunch time and he wanted to know what they were having.

"We are having sandwiches. We are having soup," Cook said when he asked.

"Uh, we're having both then?" Luke asked.

"We are having sandwiches. We are having soup," Ellen repeated.

"This is getting so annoying," Luke complained. "Everyone's talking like Kirk's robot!" Luke thought about what he'd said. "Something's wrong. I have to get Father to listen to me!" Luke left and found his father still reading the paper in the sunroom.

"Father, everyone is speaking like Kirk's robot!" Luke exclaimed.

"I like that Kirk's robot brings drinks. I like that Kirk's robot brings snacks," the king said, not looking up from his paper.

"Right! I like that too, but there's a problem."

"Kirk worked hard. Kirk programmed his robot to speak."

"Yes, he did," Luke said, "but there's a problem."

"You are jealous. You are good at many things, too," the king said.

"No, I'm not jealous! That's not the problem," Luke insisted.

"I will finish my paper. I will workout," the king said.

"See? *That's* the problem!" Luke was so frustrated that he left the room. He found Comet and poured his heart out to him. "At least you're not talking like a robot," he said, cuddling him. He had a

140

thought. "You're not the only one who won't talk like a robot, Comet!" He stood up quickly and ran to the library, with Comet barking and chasing him.

Once in the library, Luke asked Screen for a status report. Nothing appeared out of the ordinary. "But something is broken. I know it," Luke said. "Screen, is anything in the galaxy broken? Like not working?" Soon Screen showed Luke a picture of Conjunction Station with a closed sign in front of it. "Conjunction Station. Hm," Luke wondered aloud. He removed the guidebook from the shelf in the library and looked up conjunctions. He read the entry.

Conjunctions
Conjunctions join words, parts of sentences, and complete sentences together. Conjunctions can create longer sentences from short ones. For example, *I am hot. I am thirsty.* becomes *I am hot and thirsty.* The most common conjunctions are **and**, **but**, and **or**.

"I am hot. I am thirsty. That's how my family sounds! They are talking like robots because there are no conjunctions. Screen, what happens at Conjunction Station?" Luke asked.

Screen responded by playing a video. "Here at Conjunction Station," a woman reported, "words, parts of sentences, and even complete sentences are connected with conjunctions. Conjunction Station is a vital part of making planet Sentence work."

"So without Conjunction Station in operation, we will all sound like robots. We need *and*, *but*, and *or*. Comet, we have to tell everyone what's going on." Luke and Comet ran to explain the problem to his family.

★ ★ ★ ★ ★ ★ ★ ★ ★ ★

initiative – *lead*

★ ★ ★ ★ ★ ★ ★ ★ ★ ★

The king congratulated Luke for taking **initiative** with the problem. And he apologized for not listening to him. He said most likely the Gremlin had managed to have Conjunction Station closed. He said he would contact the Galactic Railroad Administration to have it reopened immediately. "That won't fix the sentences that didn't get a conjunction, however. I want you to go to planet Sentence. I want you to add conjunctions to sentences," the king said. The children agreed and left after they created a mission called Combining Short Sentences.

What does *overindulge* mean?

What is a conjunction?

Why was everyone speaking like a robot?

Chapter 28

"Are you ready for the PWA?" the queen asked her children at breakfast.

"Mother, you're using an acronym," Kirk teased.

"I guess I am," the queen said, laughing. "Are you ready for the Planetary Writing Assessment? Acronyms do save time, don't they?"

The three English children nodded and smiled.

Luke took a big bite of English muffin and started answering. When his mother frowned, he finished chewing first. "I think I'm ready."

"That's marvelous," the king said. "Kirk and Ellen?"

The two agreed they were also ready.

"I'm glad my children are eager to take the exam. Nothing pleases me more than to see children writing well."

After breakfast, the three of them walked to the main library branch. It was one of many test locations. "After the test, do you want to play catch with me, Kirk?" Luke asked.

Kirk was hoping to do some programming but said he would. His parents encouraged them to spend time together when they could. Ellen said she already had plans to go to a friend's.

Once they were seated in a library classroom, they were given the test instructions. Kirk was relieved that everything went smoothly with that part of the exam. He had considered the possibility of the Gremlin interfering.

Kirk was able to ask his siblings how it was going during a break. Both felt they were doing fine. Kirk was relieved once again.

When the three walked home, they were in high spirits. The exam was behind them and a whole Saturday afternoon was in front of them.

A month later, the king requested his family's presence in the library. The children were wondering what was going on. Was there a crisis? The queen did not seem to know the purpose of the meeting, either.

"I know you're wondering what this is all about," the king started. He held up three forms. "These are your PWA results." Kirk, Luke, and Ellen looked alarmed.

"Is it bad news?" Luke asked, trembling a little.

"I'll say it is!" the king was trying not to lose his temper. The queen encouraged him to calm down.

"It can't be that bad. Our children are good writers," the queen said.

"That's what I thought," the king said, his voice rising. "Now I think you've been spending too much time playing video games and not enough time writing."

"We haven't!" Ellen argued, ready to cry. "We do a lot of copywork."

"I really haven't seen them playing a lot of video games, dear," the queen defended them.

"I don't know how you explain these then," the king said, throwing the reports on the table.

Each of the children picked up a report and reviewed it. Ellen's lips trembled and her eyes filled with tears. "I don't understand it. I felt like I knew what I was doing." The queen put her arm around Ellen to comfort her.

Kirk said, "I feel the same way."

"Me, too!" Luke added.

"Well, we've failed, dear. The royal English children can't write," the king said with **resignation**.

The queen picked up Ellen's report and

★ ★ ★ ★ ★ ★ ★ ★ ★ ★

resignation – *acceptance*

distinguishing – *deciding*

★ ★ ★ ★ ★ ★ ★ ★ ★ ★

scanned it. "Ellen's report suggests that she wasn't **distinguishing** between sentence fragments and complete sentences. Kirk, can I see yours?"

After the queen reviewed Kirk's report, she declared that he had the same issue. When she finished looking over Luke's report, she said, "It's the same problem for all three of them."

144

"It's still embarrassing. Our children don't know the difference between a fragment and a sentence? Intolerable!" The king's **rant** was interrupted by an alert on

★ ★ ★ ★ ★ ★ ★ ★ ★ ★

rant – *yelling*

★ ★ ★ ★ ★ ★ ★ ★ ★ ★

his communicator. He read the message to his family. "There is a developing story. Students across the planet failed the Planetary Writing Assessment. Parents are upset. They are demanding improvements in the planet's education."

The king was astonished. "None of our students know the difference between a fragment and a sentence?"

"Father, the results of the PWA were fine last year, correct?" Kirk asked.

The king thought for a moment. "Yes. I don't recall any problems. What are you thinking?"

"Could something be happening on planet Sentence that would explain these results?"

The king hung his head. "Yes, of course, it could. Before we investigate, I want to apologize to you three. I should have thought before I reacted."

The children were quick to offer forgiveness.

"Screen, show me any news stories from planet Sentence," the king requested.

"There is nothing to report, Your Majesty," Screen stated after a moment.

"Nothing to report? That makes no sense," the king said.

"Maybe we should use the guidebook," Ellen suggested. When her family agreed it was a good idea, she removed the book from its shelf. She read the entry on sentence fragments aloud.

Sentences and Sentence Fragments

You can remember the rules for a sentence with this rhyme:

A sentence starts with a capital letter, my friend,
And has a period, exclamation, or question mark at the end.
A sentence needs a subject, the who or what it's about.
It also needs a verb like *is*, *go*, *sing*, or *shout*.

Instead of a sentence, it's a fragment you've got
If all the words together are not a complete thought.

A sentence fragment may begin with a capital letter and have an end mark but is missing a subject, verb, or a complete thought. For example,

The star exploded. (complete sentence)

After the star exploded. (sentence fragment, not a complete thought)

And exploded in a huge fireball. (sentence fragment, no subject, not a complete thought)

The exploding star. (sentence fragment, no verb, not a complete thought)

"Father, are words reviewed in any way on planet Sentence?" Kirk asked.

"Of course. We have patrols who assess whether words immigrating to the planet will be allowed in," the king explained.

"Do you think there's any way sentence fragments are getting past the patrols? Wouldn't that explain what is happening?" Kirk asked.

"Hm. It would explain it. I don't know why patrols aren't catching fragments, though," the king replied.

"Couldn't the Gremlin be involved?" Luke asked.

"The Gremlin could always be involved," the king admitted, groaning. "I would like you three to go to planet Sentence to investigate."

The three children expressed their excitement at the idea.

"Before we go, though, I think we should send out a mission. I hate to think of the other guardians feeling as bad as we did about the PWA results," Ellen said.

Kirk and Luke agreed. They worked together to create a sentences and fragments mission. Then they used the spaceporter to leave for planet Sentence.

What does *rant* mean?

A sentence starts with a what?

Why did the English children fail the Planetary Writing Exam?

Chapter 29

Ellen couldn't stop fidgeting and chattering with excitement. She was going to Prairie Days with her mother. The two ladies had read *Little House on the Prairie* together again to be prepared. It was a favorite for them both. Ellen had read all about the Prairie Days event being held on planet Composition. There would be nature hikes and crafts. There would be **reenactments** of early prairie dwellers. There would be homemade food and games to play. But Ellen was most excited about getting to wear her bonnet. She would look just like Laura Ingalls Wilder!

Several of her Grammar Girls friends were going with their mothers. That made it even more exciting. Ellen struggled to keep from telling her mother to hurry up.

★ ★ ★ ★ ★ ★ ★ ★ ★ ★
reenactments – *imitations*
placate – *calm*
fauna – *wildlife*
★ ★ ★ ★ ★ ★ ★ ★ ★ ★

"We'll be there in plenty of time, Ellen," her mother said to **placate** her. Ellen didn't appear to believe her. The queen agreed to take the spaceporter so Ellen wouldn't continue to complain.

The two arrived at a registration area where they met friends. Ellen and her friends spied a covered wagon and asked to visit it first. The girls climbed into the wagon, while a guide talked about what wagon travel was like in the past.

The girls and their mothers then walked nearby to see a weaving demonstration. Ellen and her friends were able to make small weavings of their own. They took turns holding up their creations to earn compliments.

A man with a clipboard came up to the women and asked if they wanted to take the Paragraph Plains tour. When they learned it was free, they signed up for the next time slot.

While they waited, they had a snack. The homemade baked goods and apple cider were pronounced delicious.

The girls were delighted when it was time for the tour. They would be riding out to Paragraph Plains in one of the covered wagons!

It was much bumpier than they had imagined. "What if you were riding in this all day?" the queen asked. The mothers murmured their agreement that it was rough. The girls shrugged and pretended to think it would still be fun.

The group passed some prairie flora and **fauna** that a guide described for them. The girls snapped photos and shared them with one another.

Finally, after a lengthy ride, they arrived at Paragraph Plains. The group's mouths hung open. As far as they could see, there were paragraphs. In fact, they couldn't see anything but paragraphs. There were so many of them, no prairie was visible. The conditions seemed to be wearing on the paragraphs. They were packed together and miserable.

It was more than the queen could take. "Excuse me," she said to the guide, "but why are there no open spaces here? I thought that's what plains were? This is more crowded than a city!"

"Oh, Your Majesty," the guide said, recognizing her, "plains used to be wide open spaces. Not anymore. We have too many paragraphs for the land reserved for them. Fortunately, paragraphs are quite adaptable."

The queen's expression suggested she didn't agree. "Thank you so much for explaining," she said. She was quiet for the rest of the trip. The wagon moved through the fields, forcing the paragraphs to shuffle and make way. The girls greeted them, feeling sorry for them.

When they returned from the plains, the whole group was gloomy. They thanked the guide, however. One of the mothers suggested they have some lemonade. It had been a hot, dry trip. Everyone agreed. They should have been refreshed after their drink. But instead, they decided to head home.

Back at the castle, Ellen's shoulders sagged. "Were you disappointed in Prairie Days, Ellen?" the queen asked.

"Oh, no! I loved all of it, except..."

"Paragraph Plains," the queen finished her sentence.

"Right."

"I know how you feel. Don't worry. I'm going to speak to your father about it."

"Really?" Ellen said, beginning to feel better.

"Of course. The conditions for those paragraphs were terrible! I doubt your father knows," the queen reassured her.

At dinner that evening, the queen and Ellen talked about their Prairie Days experience. They saved the description of Paragraph Plains for last. The king and the boys were surprised to hear of the overcrowding. The king wanted to see for himself. He asked Screen to show him pictures of it. When he saw the photos, he was angry. "This is not only mistreatment of the paragraphs but a threat to the galaxy!" he said.

"How is it a threat, Father?" Kirk asked.

The king asked that the guidebook be brought to the dining room. When it arrived, he asked Kirk to read the entry on paragraphs.

Paragraphs

A paragraph is a part of a written composition about one topic. It may also be the dialogue of one speaker. A paragraph is made up of one or more sentences.

Paragraphs begin on a new line. The first line of a paragraph is usually indented, beginning a few spaces to the right of the margin. The white space around paragraphs makes papers and books easier to read. A new paragraph in fiction can make it clear that another character is speaking.

A good nonfiction paragraph includes a topic sentence, supporting sentences, and a concluding sentence. The topic sentence is usually the first sentence. It explains what the rest of the paragraph will be about. Supporting sentences give more information about the topic. A concluding sentence usually summarizes what has been said. It can also tell what happened.

"Will overcrowding in Paragraph Plains make books harder to read?" Ellen asked.

"And harder to know which character is speaking in a book?" Luke asked.

"Yes, that's exactly right. When we look at pages of text with no white space, we don't even want to read them," the king said.

"So, I should use lots of white space when I write papers?" Luke asked.

"There's such a thing as too much white space, too, Luke," the king said, grinning.

"What are we going to do about the paragraphs, Father?" Ellen asked, her eyes brimming with tears. "They looked so miserable."

The king put his arm around his daughter. "Don't you worry, Ellen. I'm going to expand the boundaries of Paragraph Plains right away. Those paragraphs will have plenty of room again."

Ellen hugged her father and thanked him.

"I think we still have a problem," Kirk said. When the rest of the family asked him what it was, he explained. "I didn't know how important white space is in writing. I wasn't even that sure about what a paragraph was. If the guardians aren't sure either, couldn't Paragraph Plains become overcrowded again?"

"Son, I am proud of you. You're right! You three need to send out a mission on paragraphs," the king said.

The three English children got to work immediately.

What does *fauna* mean?

Why was Ellen sad about her Prairie Days trip?

What is one problem with overcrowding in Paragraph Plains?

Chapter 30

The king came into the media room in the evening. He found Kirk watching the news. "You know your mother and I don't like you watching the news without **supervision**. Some stories aren't appropriate and others are too biased," the king said.

"I know. I have to do it for a writing assignment."

"Oh. Very well then. I'll watch with you."

"Great!" Kirk had a pen and notebook, ready to take notes.

A news anchor began, "First story top tonight our traffic are." She shook her head and tried again. "Story air tonight top is our traffic." She frowned and her co-anchor stared at her.

"We seem to be having some technical difficulties. We'll go to a commercial and we'll be right back."

An ad's music began playing loudly. "Who do they have to increase the volume for commercials?" the king complained.

"To get our attention, I suppose," Kirk answered.

"Do you have to watch the news on this network?" the king asked. "Their teleprompter must be **malfunctioning**."

"I can watch any network," Kirk answered. The king asked Screen to show another news program.

A male anchor was speaking. "Much too are teens communicators using?" The anchor cleared his throat and tried again. "Using teens much are too communicators? We seem to be having a problem with our teleprompter. My apologies. We'll take a break and be right back."

"Uh-oh," Kirk said. "Has the Gremlin **tampered** with the teleprompters?"

Luke came into the media room. "You watching what are? I mean, watching you are what?"

Kirk and the king looked at one another. "Teleprompters not the it's."

"Right," the king agreed.

"Now what?" Kirk asked.

The king asked Screen for a news report. He scrolled through stories until he came to a story on the retirement of the famous Maestro. He touched the screen to play the video.

A man in a tuxedo was leaving Order Hall on planet Sentence. A narrator was saying how many years the Maestro had been conducting word order on the planet. He continued by saying he had suddenly decided to quit without explanation. No suitable replacement had been found, the narrator said.

"Good is this not," the king said.

"See I that can," Kirk answered.

"Back have we him get to," Luke said. His brother and father nodded.

Kirk used his communicator to search for the Maestro's contact information. When he found it, he placed a call to him. "Unknown number," his communicator reported.

"Has somewhere to he be," Kirk said. "Screen, Maestro."

Screen understood that Kirk wanted more information on the Maestro. A number of stories were produced on the conductor. Kirk found one about his personal life that included a video. He touched it to play it.

The Maestro was being interviewed in his cabin in the Grammarese Mountains. "This is where I come to be inspired," the Maestro said. "Ordering words is an art. When I spend a little time here, words just seem to fall into place."

"He where that's is," Kirk said. "Screen, location?"

Screen showed the location of the cabin on the map. "Go let's!" Luke said.

"Ellen tell let's," Kirk agreed.

The two managed to communicate to their sister what was happening, despite the confusing way they spoke. The three guardians used the spaceporter to go to the remote cabin. They knocked on the door.

The Maestro answered and recognized them immediately. "Why are you here?" he asked.

The children were relieved they could speak normally. "Why did you quit conducting at Order Hall?" Kirk asked.

The Maestro's shoulders sagged. "Wait a minute. I'll show you." He invited them in and brought Kirk a letter. Kirk read it out loud.

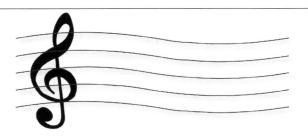

Maestro:

We are grateful for your years of service at Order Hall. To show our appreciation, we are offering you this early retirement package. If you retire now, we will give you a generous gift.

Signed, Patrons of Order Hall

"I couldn't believe it," the Maestro said emotionally. "I'm too young to retire. I love conducting the words. But I knew when I got that letter that I wasn't wanted anymore. So I quit."

"I'm sorry," Ellen said sympathetically.

"Me, too," Luke said.

"Yes. I can see how upsetting that letter would be. But I think it's a fake," Kirk said.

"What? Who would send me a fake letter?" the Maestro asked.

"The Gremlin," the three answered in unison.

"Your absence has resulted in words being out of order on our planet. We need you! No one wants you to retire."

"Are you sure?" the Maestro asked, beginning to be encouraged.

"I know the king doesn't want you to retire," Kirk reassured him.

"I'll return immediately," the Maestro said. The children thanked him and returned to the castle.

Upon their return, they did their best to explain what had happened with their words still out of order. The king had them each read the entry in the guidebook called "Word Order."

Word Order
Words in sentences should be in an order that makes sense. Most English sentences begin with the subject that is followed by the verb. For example, *The king did eat.* rather than *Ate, the king did.*

""Help the we guardians' need," Ellen said.

Luke nodded and said, "Order get back to in the words."

Kirk and Ellen didn't really understand. But they knew they needed the guardians to help get words back in order. Before they sent out a word order mission, they had it sent to the Maestro, who made sure it was in order.

What does *tampered* mean?

What comes first in most English sentences, the subject or the verb?

Why were the words out of order?

156

Chapter 31

The king was having a tennis lesson with all three children on their outdoor courts. It gave the queen time to watch one of her favorite shows: *Author Hour*. She was looking forward to the interview with the author of a mystery series she had been reading.

The host of *Author Hour* also seemed to be a fan of the author she was interviewing. "I've read every book of yours!" she gushed.

The author seemed a little embarrassed by the host's enthusiasm. "That's wonderful," she replied graciously.

The two discussed how she got started writing. The host also asked where she found her inspiration. Finally, she asked the author about the next book in the series. "Can you give us any hints?" she asked.

"Oh, you know I'm not allowed to do that," the author chuckled nervously.

"I promise not to tell anyone," the host said, winking at the audience. When the author just laughed, she continued. "So seriously. You can tell us when the next book will be released, right? How far along are you in the book?"

"Uh, I don't have an exact date yet. And I'm making progress. For sure. I mean—I'm sure I'll finish it soon. It's just—." The author's hands shook and she seemed incredibly anxious.

"Have you had personal or health issues that have gotten in the way?" the host asked sympathetically. "I'm sure we can relate, right?" she asked the audience.

"Uh, no, actually. I wish! That would be a lot easier to explain," the author said, looking down at her lap.

"You're not saying what I think you're saying?" the host asked dramatically. "Do you have writer's block?"

"No! I mean—I don't think so. Maybe?" the author squeaked out.

"How long has it been since you've written anything?"

"On the book?" the author asked to stall.

"Yes, on the book."

"Um, I would say—three maybe?"

"Three weeks?" the host asked.

"Nooo." She paused. "Three months," the author admitted.

The host and the audience gasped. "You realize that's writer's block," the host said.

"Yes," the author said, beginning to cry quietly. The host patted her hand and reassured her she would be past it soon.

When the show cut to commercial, the queen thought out loud, "Writer's block? Her? That's not good. Not good at all."

The king and the children came back to the house after their tennis lesson. They were laughing and **boisterous**.

★ ★ ★ ★ ★ ★ ★ ★ ★ ★

boisterous – *energetic*

feigning – *faking*

★ ★ ★ ★ ★ ★ ★ ★ ★ ★

The queen called the king aside. "I have to tell you about *Author Hour.*"

"Ah, yes. I'm sure it was good," the king said, distracted.

"No, it wasn't. You know the author of that mystery series I love?"

The king nodded, though he really couldn't recall.

"She was on the show. And guess what?"

"What?" the king said, **feigning** attention.

"She has writer's block," the queen announced. That got the king's attention.

"Writer's block? How long?"

"Three months," the queen answered.

"Three months? Hm. Who did you say the author was again?"

"You weren't listening!" The queen was annoyed but repeated what she'd said.

"Recently a best seller?" the king asked. When the queen nodded, the king added, "That's not writer's block. It's fame **aversion**. She doesn't want to be famous. And who can blame her? It's a hard life."

★ ★ ★ ★ ★ ★ ★ ★ ★ ★

aversion – *dislike*

★ ★ ★ ★ ★ ★ ★ ★ ★ ★

"I don't think that's what it is. I really think it's writer's block," the queen argued.

"It's *her* writer's block, dear. I don't believe this is a risk." The king smiled at his wife. He asked the children if they wanted a cold drink and left with them to find one.

After a few days, the queen had convinced herself that her husband was right. She had heard of no other cases of writer's block. But she noticed an article on the front page of the lifestyle section of *The Grammar Gazette*.

The article mentioned that a top publisher had dropped one of its best-selling authors. He had failed to produce a book on schedule. The author was quoted as saying he wanted to finish the book but just couldn't.

"Writer's block," the queen whispered. She showed the article to her husband, who remained unconvinced there was a problem.

"He probably didn't want to write that particular book. You know how publishers are. They wanted a title they thought would sell and he said yes. Then he changed his mind."

The king's response reassured the queen. It probably wasn't an epidemic of writer's block. But something made her continue to investigate.

She found Ellen in her room. "What are you up to today, dear?" the queen asked.

"I'm writing a story," she replied proudly.

"That's wonderful!" the queen exclaimed. She was relieved. But her relief didn't last for long. At dinner, both Kirk and Luke seemed out of sorts. The queen asked them if they'd had a bad day. Both replied that they were struggling with a writing assignment.

The king overheard and asked if they hadn't understood the assignment. Both boys said they had understood. They even started writing a story but weren't able to write any more.

The queen's eyes grew wide as she sought her husband's. "It's writer's block," she said.

"Now, we don't know that," the king answered.

"Cases of it are starting to pile up," the queen argued.

"What's writer's block again?" Luke asked.

"It's when writers get stuck and don't know what to write," the king answered.

"Yes, and we've had epidemics of it in the galaxy before. If this is another one, we need to act quickly to keep it from spreading. Otherwise, we'll have thousands of unfinished stories and books," the queen answered.

"I definitely have writer's block!" Luke declared.

"Me, too!" added Kirk. "And all my friends have it, too," he said, holding up his communicator as proof.

The queen gave the king a look as if to say, "I told you so."

"But I don't have it," Ellen interjected.

"That's right," the queen said. "Why wouldn't she have it if it's an epidemic?"

"She must have immunity," the king said. "She's doing things that prevent her from getting it."

"What things?" Ellen asked.

"We need the guidebook to answer that. Let's all go to the library and read it together," the king suggested.

Writer's Block
Writer's block is difficulty knowing what to write. Often it occurs because the writer wants the work to be perfect. Or, the writer fears having the writing judged. Writer's block can be worse when there is time pressure. To cure writer's block (or be immune to it), write without judging the work. Don't think about what other people will think of your writing. Write anything, even if it isn't related to the project. For example, write about writer's block. Then

work on your project again. Or instead of writing, work on the outline or plan for the project. You can try reading for inspiration. Also, be sure to start early on a writing project and work consistently.

"Ellen, don't you worry what people will think of your stories?" Luke asked.

"No. I just have fun with it. I still get nervous about speaking, though," she admitted.

"We need to share the information about the cure for writer's block as soon as possible," Kirk said.

"Yes, but we still have a problem," the queen warned. "Until everyone is cured, we have all kinds of unfinished stories and books."

"We could send the cure to the guardians and have the guardians finish them," the king suggested.

Everyone agreed that was a great idea. "But I'm not sure how to finish a story," Luke said.

"Luke, remember when we completed a mission on story action? There's exposition, rising action, a climax, falling action, and a resolution. Whatever hasn't been written, we can add," Kirk explained.

"So I can decide how the story ends? That could be fun!" Luke said.

The three English children worked on a mission called Story Completion. They had it sent to the guardians right away.

What does *feigning* mean?

What is writer's block?

Why didn't Ellen have writer's block?

Chapter 32

The queen was a little late picking up Ellen from her Grammar Girls meeting. "I got so into my book," she said, apologizing. Mrs. G., the group leader, said not to worry about it. That happened to her all the time. Ellen didn't seem to mind, either. She was so excited to talk about the meeting.

"I have to write a research paper!" Ellen explained on the walk home.

"You do? Were you given a topic?" the queen asked.

"No, but I know what I want to write about. Arabian horses!" she announced.

"Wonderful! I know you love horses. Did she give you any special instructions for writing the paper?"

"Yes. We have to use an encyclopedia to do the research. And I can't use Screen," Ellen said, looking disappointed.

The queen smiled. "That will be a good experience, Ellen. Did she say you couldn't use encyclopedias online?"

"No. We can use them. We just can't ask Screen to do all the work for us." The two of them laughed as she said it.

That evening Ellen looked up Arabian horses in an online encyclopedia. She couldn't believe how much information there was on them. It would take her all night to read it all! She only needed enough information to write a short paper. Mrs. G. mentioned that she could use a print encyclopedia to do the research, too. She decided to go to the library to look the next day.

When Ellen found an entry on Arabian horses in the A volume of their encyclopedia, she was shocked. There was just as much information! She didn't want to read all of that.

Then she remembered that there was a children's encyclopedia in their library. She hoped it would help her find just the right information to write her report. But when she looked for Arabian horses, there was no entry. She did find an entry on horses, but she wanted to write specifically on the Arabian breed.

Ellen thought about asking her mother for help. But she really wanted to write the paper herself. She knew her mother would be so proud of her first research paper. She told herself that she would figure out what to do later.

As the days went by, Ellen thought about the paper. She remembered how frustrated she was trying to use the encyclopedia. Once again, she decided to work on it later.

Before she knew it, she only had two days left to write her paper. Ellen was relieved that her mother hadn't been asking about it. She wouldn't want to lie to her. Apparently, her mother had forgotten about the assignment. Ellen tried to decide what to do. She didn't want to disappoint her mother by admitting she hadn't started the paper. She didn't want to disappoint Mrs. G. by not doing the paper. But she had no idea how to use the encyclopedia to write it. Finally, she told herself that it would be okay to get Screen's help with this first paper. Even so, she went to her room and talked to Screen via her tablet. She hoped she wouldn't be disturbed.

"Screen, I need two pages of information about Arabian horses. In plain English, please," Ellen requested. Just then she heard a knock at the door.

"Ellen, are you asking Screen for help with your paper?" the queen asked before opening the door. "You aren't done with it yet?"

Ellen hung her head in shame. "No," she whispered.

"I can't believe you used Screen when you were specifically forbidden to do so!" The queen shouted and Ellen **recoiled**. "And you procrastinated, too. What will Mrs. G. think?" The queen's cheeks flushed.

★ ★ ★ ★ ★ ★ ★ ★ ★ ★

recoiled – *withdrew*

jocular – *funny*

★ ★ ★ ★ ★ ★ ★ ★ ★ ★

The king appeared in the open doorway. "Hey, what's all the shouting about?" he asked in a **jocular** way. His expression grew serious when he saw how angry the queen was. "Oh. What's wrong?"

The queen explained that Ellen hadn't started her research paper. And she had broken the rules. "Ellen, would you like to explain?" the king asked her.

Ellen began to sob. She was heartbroken that she had disappointed her parents. "I—I—tried to use the online encyclopedia. But—but—there was so much. I—I—couldn't even read it all. So I—I—used the encyclopedia in the library—"

"That was smart," the king said, urging her to continue.

"But there was just as much in there," she said before wailing even more loudly.

"There, there," the king said, putting his arm around her. "It's not so bad."

"Not so bad?" the queen cried. "She is a princess and a guardian, too!" The queen looked as though she would join her daughter in crying soon.

"Ellen, do you know how to use an encyclopedia to do research?" the king asked.

"No!" Ellen sobbed. She buried her face in her hands and her shoulders shook as she cried.

The king looked at the queen sternly. "Dear, the child hasn't been taught how to do research. What do you expect?"

"You're not blaming me for this, are you?" The queen was furious.

"No, no!" the king said, alarmed at the turn the conversation was taking. "I'm simply saying that she used Screen because she didn't know what else to do."

"Yes! That's right," Ellen said, regaining her pride a little.

"That's no excuse," the queen chided her. "If you needed help, you should have asked."

Ellen was silent for a moment. "You're right, Mother. I'm sorry."

"Oh, this is good. I can't stand seeing you two upset," the king said.

The queen accepted Ellen's apology and the two hugged one another.

"It's clear what we need to do now," the king announced. He called for the two boys and the guidebook. When he had them in place, he read the entry on Encyclopedias.

Encyclopedias

An encyclopedia is a book or series of books that gives information on a variety of subjects. The subjects are listed in alphabetical order. An encyclopedia can also be a searchable website.

To find information on a person, <u>search for the person's last name</u>. For example, search for Abraham Lincoln under L. To find the name of a place, <u>search for the first word in the place name</u>. For example, search for Rhode Island under R. To search for a topic, <u>search the most important word in the topic, unless it is too broad</u>. For example, search for deep sea fishing under F for fishing.

A children's encyclopedia makes doing research easier for students. The first paragraph on a subject may provide the most important information. After that, the subheadings or topics in bold will help you find the facts you are looking for. Subheadings can be used to organize a paper or further research. Many encyclopedia entries refer to other articles that may be helpful using "see also."

In an encyclopedia entry on **soccer**, the subheadings might include history, laws, and competitions. A paper could include something on each subtopic or could focus on just one of these. Take notes from the encyclopedia article. Do not copy the encyclopedia sentences word for word.

See also **Citation**.

"It seems like the guidebook is an encyclopedia," Luke said.

"Smart boy," the king declared, patting him on the back. "It's an encyclopedia of Grammar Galaxy."

★ ★ ★ ★ ★ ★ ★ ★ ★ ★

citation – *reference*

★ ★ ★ ★ ★ ★ ★ ★ ★ ★

"Do you have to use citation for your paper, Ellen?" the queen asked.

"No. Mrs. G. just wanted us to learn to use the encyclopedia. And write a short paper, of course," Ellen answered.

"Yes, there is time for you to learn about that later. But there's not much time left for you to write this paper. Listen, I have something that will help you take notes from the encyclopedia," the queen said.

Ellen felt much better about the project. She found she was excited to try using the encyclopedia again. "There's just one problem," she said. "If I don't know how to use an encyclopedia, do you think the guardians may not know?"

"Ellen, I'm proud of you for thinking of them. We definitely need to send out a mission, don't we, boys?" the king said.

The two agreed and worked with Ellen to send out a mission they called Encyclopedias.

What does *jocular* mean?

Why did Ellen use Screen to cheat on her paper?

Using what letter would you search an encyclopedia for information on <u>Abraham Lincoln?</u>

Chapter 33

"Ellen, you received a letter from the Poetry Society. Hurry and open it. I can't wait to see what it's about," the queen said. While Ellen began opening the letter, the queen said she loved poetry. "Read it out loud, Ellen," she urged her.

"Your Highness, Miss Ellen English, we were so impressed with your poetry reading last year. We would be honored if you would write a poem to present at our annual convention. We are hoping in particular that you will submit a shape poem. This new style of poetry has become so popular with young people. Would you have it prepared for display in the convention hall? Our committee is wanting it to be the **hallmark** of the event. We will be eagerly anticipating it. Sincerely, the Poetry Society Convention Committee. P.S. Could you have it sent at your earliest convenience?"

★ ★ ★ ★ ★ ★ ★ ★ ★ ★

hallmark – *symbol*

queasy – *sick*

predicament – *difficulty*

★ ★ ★ ★ ★ ★ ★ ★ ★ ★

"Oh, Ellen, what an honor!" the queen gushed. "I have never been asked to submit poetry to the society. I wonder why. No matter. My own daughter has been asked to share her poetry! And it will be on display for the entire convention to see."

Ellen felt **queasy**. She wasn't a poet. And what's more, she had no idea what a shape poem was. But her mother was so excited.

"You'll need a new gown. And you should wear your hair up. Everyone will want to greet you. You're practically the poet laureate," the queen said.

"What's a poet laureate?" Ellen asked.

"It's an honorary position for a poet. He or she represents a nation or in your case, a planet."

"But they didn't say anything about me being poet laureate," Ellen said, feeling annoyed. "I'm not even a plain poet!"

"Oh, Ellen, you will be in time. I'm sure of it." The queen immediately contacted one of her friends via communicator. "You won't believe it," she said. "Ellen's going to be the poet laureate!"

Ellen couldn't help but remind her mother that she had just been asked to write a shape poem.

"Exactly! That's the first step," the queen said, returning to her call.

Ellen walked to her bedchamber forlornly. *How could she possibly get out of this horrible **predicament**?* she wondered. Especially when her mother was so excited. Could she pretend to be sick? No. She would have to pretend for weeks. Could she fake a hand injury? She couldn't do that, either. Her mother would offer to write while Ellen dictated. Could she have Screen find her a shape poem? No. She'd tried cheating before and that hadn't gone well.

Then she suddenly knew what to do: she would read the guidebook! She could learn how to write a shape poem on her own.

168

She would write it and she would make her mother proud. Just as suddenly, she remembered something and reread the letter. It said that shape poems were a new style of poetry. There wouldn't be anything in the guidebook about it!

Ellen was discouraged. She laid back on her bed and worried about what to do. She woke up an hour later. She had needed the rest. It helped her think clearly. Her father had told them that if they needed help, they should ask. Well, she definitely needed help!

Ellen found her mother in her study. She planned to tell her that she didn't know what a shape poem was. The queen was excited to see her only daughter. "Have you been thinking about the topic of your poem?" she asked.

"Not exactly," Ellen started.

"I understand. It's normal to be thinking about what you'll wear. It's normal to think about whom you'll meet and invite, too," the queen said dreamily.

"I wasn't thinking about that, either," Ellen said.

"Are you worried about getting it done right away? Don't," the queen reassured her.

"Really?" Ellen said, a little relieved.

"Really. They won't need it right away. You're the princess, so they know you will finish it and do a fabulous job, too."

"Uh—," Ellen started. She planned to admit that she had no idea how to write a shape poem. But her mother had said she had plenty of time. So instead she said, "Thanks for being so excited for me, Mother."

The queen rose to hug her daughter. "Of course I'm excited! And I just realized something else I can do to help. Poets need inspiration. I'm going to take you someplace surrounded by nature. Don't you worry about a thing. I'll take care of everything." She smiled and patted Ellen on the back as she left the room.

Ellen had an uneasy feeling in her stomach. But she told herself her mother was right. She could definitely use some inspiration. And while she and her mother were away, she could admit that she had no idea how to write a shape poem.

At dinner that evening, the queen couldn't stop talking about the poem Ellen was going to write. "I'm going to take her somewhere gorgeous and peaceful."

"Why?" the king asked. "Why do you have to go away? She can write the poem right here."

"Don't be ridiculous," the queen said, insulted. "All the great poets were inspired by nature."

"Is Ellen a great poet?" Luke whispered to Kirk. Kirk shrugged to say he didn't know.

"How long will you be away? And more importantly, how much will this little trip cost?" the king asked suspiciously.

"It doesn't matter how much it costs," the queen said, her voice rising. "This is an opportunity of a lifetime." Her cheeks were red with anger and it scared Ellen.

"May I please be excused?" Ellen asked.

"Me, too?" the boys asked. The children didn't want to hear their parents arguing.

Later, in the media room, Kirk asked Ellen if she felt she had to be in nature to write her poem. "I could be in the most amazing place in the galaxy, but I still wouldn't know how to write a shape poem. Do you know how? Please tell me you do!"

"Sorry, I have no idea," Kirk said. "Did you tell Mother you don't know how to write one?"

"I planned to. But she is so excited. I hoped to tell her once we were alone together," Ellen explained.

The queen interrupted them when she walked into the room. She looked as though she had been crying. "Ellen, I need to speak with you," she said. Ellen went into the hallway with her. She seemed as upset as Ellen could remember. "Your Father doesn't want us to go away for you to write your poem. I disagree, but I have to honor his wishes. I'm afraid you'll have to write the poem at home."

"Oh, Mother, I'm sorry you're disappointed," Ellen said. "But I have to tell you something."

"Not now, Ellen. I need to be alone." The queen walked away sniffling.

Ellen returned to the media room and told the boys what their mother had said. "Now what do I do?"

"Well, you can't tell her now," Kirk said.

"Obviously," Ellen said. "I would hate to upset her even more."

"Let her get some sleep. You can talk to her tomorrow."

"Yes. That's a good idea," Ellen said.

But the next day, the queen didn't come to breakfast. Cook told the family that she wasn't feeling up to it. Ellen glanced at Kirk to communicate her worry.

After breakfast, Kirk had an idea for Ellen. "Talk to Father about it. He isn't as emotional about the Poetry Society."

"Hm. That's true," Ellen said. "But do you think Father knows anything about new poetry styles?"

"Doubtful," Kirk laughed. "But I know he will help you."

The king was harsh with Ellen when she asked to come into his study. "I know your mother is upset. But don't try to change my mind. I don't think it's necessary for you to travel to write a poem!"

"That's not what I wanted to talk with you about," Ellen said, near tears.

"What then?" the king said, softening. "I'm sorry. What is it?"

"The problem isn't inspiration. The problem is—, is—." Ellen started weeping, but was able to say between sobs, "I don't know how to write a shape poem."

"A shape poem? You have to write a shape poem?"

"Yes, and I know you don't know what it is, but—." The king's laughter interrupted her. "What's so funny?" Ellen asked. She was irritated by her father making fun of her.

"You think I don't know what a shape poem is? Why, because it's the new thing? Shape poems have been around for centuries!"

"They have? Do you mean there is information about them in the guidebook then?" Ellen asked.

"Of course there is."

"So I've been worried for nothing. Thank you, Father. I'm going to go look up shape poems in the guidebook. Then hopefully I can write one."

Ellen went to the library, found the entry, and read it to herself.

Shape Poems
Shape poems (also called concrete or visual poems) have an appearance that communicates a message.

The poem may be written in the shape of the subject of the poem. For example, a poem about trees may be written in the shape of a tree. Fonts (text styles) or direction of text may also be used to give meaning to the poem. For example, the word *big* may be written in large type.

To write a shape poem, first draw or print the shape of your choice. Then write the poem to make the words fill up the shape.

"This poem doesn't rhyme!" Ellen said aloud. "That's right. I remember that not all poems have to rhyme. I think I understand what a shape poem is now. But I bet I'm not the only one who doesn't know how to write one. We need to send out a mission." She went to get her brothers to help her send out a mission called Shape Poems.

What does *predicament* mean?

Are shape poems a new way of writing poetry?

Why was Ellen worried about writing a shape poem?

Chapter 34

Lights flashed in the English kids' faces as they talked with reporters. The three of them would take part in a new program. It was called the Intergalactic Communication Project. Kids from different planets in the galaxy would be pen pals.

"I'm hoping for a pen pal who likes to cook," Ellen said shyly.

"I'd love to write to a boy who likes spaceball," Luke said.

"Writing to someone who shares my interests in robotics would be terrific," Kirk added.

The king addressed the reporters. "We are hopeful for improved relationships and understanding between planets of other languages."

A reporter asked, "Speaking of other languages, how will the students understand their letters?"

"Great question," the king said. "The letters will be mailed to the Intergalactic Communication Project headquarters. There the letters will be translated into the **recipient**'s language."

★ ★ ★ ★ ★ ★ ★ ★ ★ ★

recipient – *receiver*

★ ★ ★ ★ ★ ★ ★ ★ ★ ★

"It sounds like a great program. Would we be able to interview your children again after they receive their first letter?" asked one reporter.

"Certainly!" the king replied. "They would be glad to talk with you, wouldn't you, children?" Kirk, Luke, and Ellen agreed that they'd be honored.

A week later, they each received a letter from the Intergalactic Communication Project. It noted their pen pals' name, planet, and the instructions for participating in the project. The children were excited to share their pen pal information with one another.

"My pen pal is from planet Italy," Ellen said. "I wonder if she likes spaghetti."

"Mine's from planet Mexico," Luke said. "Maybe he owns a chihuahua!"

"Mine is from planet China," Kirk shared. "I hope he likes computers."

The three shared the questions they had for their pen pals at dinner that evening. The king and queen were thrilled that they were so enthusiastic about writing letters.

"I wonder what questions she'll have for me," Ellen said. "Maybe she'll want to know what it's like to be an English princess."

"Yeah," Luke said. "My pen pal might ask me what it's like to be a prince. But I don't know what it's like *not* to be a prince." The king and queen chuckled.

"Maybe they'll want to know what it's like being guardians," Kirk suggested.

The children had trouble sleeping that night. They kept thinking about their pen pals and what they would write.

The next day was a Saturday, so they had time to work on their letters. Kirk looked at the letter he received from the Project again. "Your letter must be in the proper format," Kirk read aloud. *What's the proper format?* he wondered. He didn't want to shame his entire family by sending a letter that wasn't written correctly. His interest in getting started on the letter **waned**. He decided to work on a new coding project instead.

★ ★ ★ ★ ★ ★ ★ ★ ★ ★

waned – *decreased*

★ ★ ★ ★ ★ ★ ★ ★ ★ ★

Ellen was excited about writing her pen pal. But she was even more excited about something else: guinea pigs. One of her friends had two guinea pigs and Ellen thought they were adorable. She had checked out a book about them from the library. She wanted to learn all about them. Then hopefully she could convince her parents to let her have guinea pigs. She planned to spend the day reading.

Luke wanted to write a letter to his pen pal. But he was really looking forward to playing spaceball with his friends. It was too nice a day to stay inside. He knew his father would agree. He did give him permission to go.

The three were distracted by their regular activities for several days. When Ellen remembered that she had to write a letter, she asked Kirk if he had started. "No," Kirk admitted. "I read the letter from the Project and it said it has to be in the proper format."

"It does?" Ellen said. "I don't remember that part."

"Yes. And the problem is I don't know what the proper format is. Do you?"

"No. Does it matter?"

"The media wants to do a story on us and our pen pals. How will it look if I don't write a letter the right way?" Kirk explained.

"I hadn't thought of that," Ellen said. "What if Luke already sent his in the wrong format?"

"I'm not worried about that," Kirk said, grinning.

The two decided to talk with Luke about his letter. Kirk was right that he hadn't started. "If we can't write the letters without the right format and we don't know the format, what should we do?" Luke asked. "Hope they forget about it?"

"Reporters are going to come interview us. They won't forget about it," Kirk said impatiently.

The butler knocked on Luke's door and announced that the children had a visitor. The three of them wondered aloud who it could be and accompanied the butler to the drawing room. The king and queen were already there.

"Children!" the queen said, "A reporter is here to interview you about your pen pal letters." She didn't seem **unnerved** that the reporter had come unexpectedly.

★ ★ ★ ★ ★ ★ ★ ★ ★ ★

unnerved – *upset*

★ ★ ★ ★ ★ ★ ★ ★ ★ ★

"Ohhh," Ellen started. "It's so nice of you to come." She hoped to distract him with her politeness.

"I hope I'm not too much of a bother," the reporter apologized.

"Well, we were really busy working on stuff," Luke said. The queen warned him with her eyes not to continue. "I mean, it's great to see you!" He shook the reporter's hand.

"Would you excuse us?" Kirk asked. "We need to speak with the king and queen privately."

"By all means," the reporter said.

The king was embarrassed by this unusual request but pretended it was entirely normal.

"What in the galaxy is going on, Kirk?" he asked when they were away from the drawing room.

"Well, we have a problem. I hope you won't be too angry," Kirk started. The king could feel himself getting tense in response. The queen told him to stay calm. Kirk continued. "We haven't exactly started our letters yet."

"What?" the king roared. The queen hushed him, so he spoke more quietly. "Why not?" he said in an angry whisper.

"I planned to write my letter right away, but I reread the letter from the Project. It said the letter has to be in the proper format. I don't know what the proper format is. I didn't want to dishonor you by sending in a letter written the wrong way," Kirk explained.

"So none of you knew the proper format for a letter?" the king asked, astonished.

Luke and Ellen shook their heads. "I don't know the proper format, but I also got distracted. I was going to write it, really I was!" Ellen said, getting emotional.

"Me, too," Luke said, hanging his head.

The king sighed. "Well, now we really have a problem, don't we? What am I going to tell the reporter?"

"How about the truth?" the queen suggested.

The king started to argue with her but changed his mind. "You're right as usual, my dear."

The king seemed more relaxed. He asked his family to accompany him back to the drawing room.

"I'm afraid you can't interview the children about their letters today," the king told the reporter. "There is something very important we have to do first. We were so eager to start the pen pal project that we forgot to teach our children how to write good letters."

"May I quote you on that?" he asked.

The king looked at the queen and smiled. "You may," he answered. "We'll be glad to have you back soon to discuss the letters."

When the reporter left, the family went to the castle library. They used the guidebook to find information on letter writing. The king said that a letter to a pen pal is called a friendly letter.

Friendly Letter Writing
Letters can be written as business letters or friendly letters. A friendly letter is written in a casual, informal style. It should include five parts: 1) Header – with the sender's address and date. 2) Greeting – usually *Dear* followed by the person's name. The greeting begins on the left of the letter, a few spaces below the header. 3) Body – the message you want to share. It is written in indented paragraphs. 4) Closing – It begins at the left of the letter. It is usually <u>Sincerely</u>, <u>Love,</u> or <u>Your friend</u> followed by a comma. 5) Signature – your name written in cursive at the left of the letter. Some letters have a postscript with extra information.

"That's the proper format for a friendly letter?" Kirk said. "Aren't the letters we send to the guardians friendly letters?"

"They're official business, so you could call them business letters. But you keep them casual, so yes. They're friendly letters," the king answered.

"I could have written my pen pal a letter right away. I thought it was more complicated," Kirk said.

"No, pretty simple," the king said.

"Even for me!" Luke exclaimed gleefully.

The king didn't smile. "I really hope you will talk to me from now on when you don't know how to do something."

"We will. We promise!" Ellen said. The boys agreed.

"Do you think other pen pals are confused about the right way to write a friendly letter?" Luke asked.

"I think it's highly likely," the king answered.

"We need to send out a mission called Friendly Letters. And we need to do it right away!" Kirk said.

What does *unnerved* mean?

Why didn't Kirk write his pen pal letter right away?

What word is usually used for a greeting in a friendly letter?

Chapter 35

Luke returned from storytelling time at the library in a good mood. The kids really seemed to enjoy his new story. He had gotten a lot more comfortable telling stories since the librarians first asked him.

He had told a story that afternoon about an alien invasion. The librarians thought it was so good that they asked him to give them a printed copy. That was a little bit of a problem. He made the story up in his head. He had practiced it a lot so he could do a good job, but he had nothing written.

He felt like putting off making a written copy. But he knew if he waited, he might forget the story. And he had to agree it was a really great one. He decided to dictate the story on his computer. He would tell it almost the same way he had to the kids, and then he would have a written copy. He was pretty proud of himself for coming up with that idea.

Comet brought him a ball as he came into the castle. "Not now, boy. Later! I have to get this story written, okay?" Comet seemed to understand. He plopped down and started trying to chew the ball.

In the computer lab, Luke pressed some keys on his computer to start his dictation program. He got an error.

"That's weird," he said. He tried it again and got the same error. He sighed deeply. "Everything takes longer than it's supposed to," he complained. "I'll have Screen help," he said.

Screen responded at the mention of his name. "Yes, Your Highness?"

"Screen, can you take dication?"

"Not at the moment. There seems to be a problem with dictation software."

"You're kidding," Luke said.

"I am not capable of kidding, Your Highness."

Luke groaned. "I know. What am I supposed to do now? I have to get this story written before I forget. How long will it take to fix the dictation problem?"

"It appears to be a **universal** and **complex** situation."

Luke thought for a moment and became concerned. "I wonder if this could be the Gremlin's doing," he said aloud. He decided to find his father and report what he'd learned.

★ ★ ★ ★ ★ ★ ★ ★ ★ ★

universal – *widespread*

complex – *difficult*

★ ★ ★ ★ ★ ★ ★ ★ ★ ★

His father was in his study speaking with a programmer. He already knew about the dictation problem. "I'm afraid the software has become corrupted. It will be quite a project to get it working again," the king warned.

"What am I supposed to do?" Luke asked. "The librarians want a typed copy of my story,"

"You'll have to type it, of course," the king said. He asked Luke to let him continue discussing the dictation software problem.

Luke was very disappointed when he left his father's study. He never typed. There had to be another way. Then it came to him. He could have his mother type his story for him while he told it. He went to look for her and finally found her in the kitchen with Cook.

"How did storytelling go?" she asked when she saw Luke.

"Great!" he exclaimed. "They really liked the alien story. They liked it so much they want a written copy of it."

"Outstanding!" the queen said. Cook congratulated him, too.

"I'm glad they liked it, but I have a problem. The Gremlin has caused problems with dictation software. So now my story has to be typed."

"It's unfortunate about the dictation software. But it's not hard to type," the queen said.

"I'd rather have you type it for me. I could tell you the story and you could type it. Couldn't you?" he begged.

"I could, but I don't have time right now. You don't need it done right now, do you?"

"Well, I'm just worried I will forget the story if I don't get it written down right away," Luke said.

"Luke, that is so mature! I'm so proud of you for not putting it off."

Luke beamed. "So you'll type it for me?"

"No."

"No? Why not?" Luke asked.

"Because you need to know how to type."

"Why do I? Before you know it, Father will have the dictation software working again," Luke said.

"But I thought you said you couldn't wait to get your story down," the queen said, smirking.

Luke knew he was defeated. "Okay," he said, sulking.

He returned to the computer lab and prepared to type out his story. "I can do this," he said to encourage himself. He used one finger of each hand to find the letters he needed. He attempted to type his story as he remembered it. But the going was so slow, he was getting confused. "This isn't going to work!" he declared. He was thoroughly frustrated.

He decided he needed a break and went looking for Comet. Playing a little fetch with him was certain to help, he thought. Before he knew it, it was time for lunch. Then he had a tennis lesson. A friend contacted him and Luke asked his mother if he could join them for dinner. His mother said yes and the two spent the evening playing ping-pong in the game room.

The next afternoon his mother thought to ask if he had his story typed. "I forgot," Luke admitted.

"Well, you had better do it or what did you say would happen?" she asked.

"I'll forget," Luke said. "It just takes sooo long," he complained.

"I'll tell you what. I'll come with you. I was once a very fast typist," she said. "I can give you tips on improving your speed."

"Or you can just type it for me," Luke said, grinning.

"Go ahead and start typing," the queen urged Luke when he was seated at the keyboard.

"Okay," Luke said, using one finger of each hand to type.

"Use all of your fingers!" the queen directed. She was surprised to see Luke typing with one finger. "Don't hunt and peck."

"I can't use all my fingers," Luke said.

"You don't know how to type?"

"Not really," he said, shaking his head.

"This is unacceptable for a young guardian."

"Dictation software is so much easier," he said.

"I understand that, but typing is a very important skill," the queen said. "This dictation software crisis proves how important it is. I want to talk with your brother and sister about this." She had Kirk and Ellen and the guidebook brought to the computer lab.

"Is this about the dictation software crisis?" Kirk asked.

"Yes and no," the queen answered. "Your brother doesn't have good keyboarding skills. He types with one finger! It takes way too long to type that way. And this

★ ★ ★ ★ ★ ★ ★ ★ ★ ★

accuracy – *exactness*

★ ★ ★ ★ ★ ★ ★ ★ ★ ★

may not be the last time we don't have access to dictation software. I want to read you this entry on keyboarding."

Keyboarding
Keyboarding is also called typing. Keyboarding speed and **accuracy** are important for most jobs. Speed and accuracy can be improved by learning to touch type. Touch typing means typing without looking at the letters on the keys. This requires memorization of the key's letters. The average typist can produce 40 words per minute (wpm). The average touch typist can produce 60 wpm. Correct position of

the hands on the keyboard can also increase typing speed and accuracy.

The most important way to increase speed and accuracy is regular practice. There are numerous programs and games that make practice more enjoyable.

To prevent overuse injuries at the keyboard, arms should be bent at 90 degrees. They should not be tilted upward or downward. The screen should be at eye level. Frequent rest breaks should be taken. Using dictation software can also prevent overuse injuries.

"See? Dictation software. It prevents injuries!" Luke proclaimed when she was finished reading.

"You need to learn how to type, Luke. Sorry," the queen said.

"So there are games we can play to learn to type faster?" Ellen said.

"Definitely!" the queen assured her.

"Fun games, though?" Luke quizzed her.

"Yes, fun games," the queen said, ruffling Luke's hair.

"I think the guardians need this information, too," Kirk said. The queen agreed. The three English children worked together on a mission called Keyboarding.

Luke asked his mother to type his story for him while he was learning to type faster. She thought that made sense.

What does *complex* mean?

Why couldn't Luke dictate his story using his computer?

What is the most important way to increase typing speed?

Chapter 36

There was an unusual level of excitement around the castle. It was the day of the king's State of the Galaxy speech. He would address the Parliament and the whole galaxy.

"Are you nervous?" Ellen asked. "I would be!"

The king laughed. "No. I'm excited," he said. "I love speaking, but I have to be prepared. It's awful to be called on to speak when you aren't ready."

"Is the galaxy in a good state?" Kirk asked.

"Yes, it is, Kirk. We've experienced a lot of crises this year, as you know. But that's to be expected. And you've handled them all so well as guardians." The king smiled at his children and hugged his wife. "We have children we can be proud of, don't we, dear?" he asked her.

"Definitely!" the queen agreed. "Now don't you need to get ready? What are you wearing? I want to look at it and make sure it's appropriate."

"You can look at it if you want to, but I'm sure I chose the right clothes," he said.

"You say that every year and every year I have to save you from embarrassing yourself," the queen teased. The couple left to go to their bedchamber.

After they'd gone, Luke asked, "Do you really think the galaxy is in a good state, Kirk?"

"Now it is. But problems seem to come up all the time. I'm worried about tonight." When his siblings asked him why, Kirk explained. "The State of the Galaxy speech would be the perfect opportunity for the Gremlin to try to embarrass Father."

"I hadn't thought of that," Luke said grimly.

"Doesn't Father have security, though?" Ellen asked.

"Of course he does. But security hasn't stopped the Gremlin from causing trouble in the past."

185

"True," Ellen admitted. "But there's nothing we can do about it, right?"

"I don't know. I think we guardians should be on high alert."

"What level of alert?" Luke asked.

"I don't know. Just high," Kirk said.

"Can't we say 'Code Red' or something like that? It sounds cool," Luke said.

Kirk sighed impatiently. "Okay. We're on a Code Red alert, Luke. But this is serious, you understand? This is one of the worst times for the Gremlin to mess things up."

"Got it," Luke said, saluting Kirk. Kirk rolled his eyes. "This situation requires special assistance. Comet and I are on it," Luke said, leaving the room.

"Didn't Father's State of the Galaxy speech go well last year?" Ellen asked.

Kirk thought a moment. "Yes. I don't remember any problems."

"See? Everything will be fine," Ellen reassured him.

In the king and queen's bedchamber, the queen was complimenting the king. "You look so **dignified**! And you look so much better than you would have in the clothes you picked out."

"Really? I thought the other suit was fine."

★ ★ ★ ★ ★ ★ ★ ★ ★ ★

dignified – *grand*

mishap – *accident*

★ ★ ★ ★ ★ ★ ★ ★ ★ ★

"Definitely not. You're fortunate you have me as your clothing consultant," the queen teased. She kissed him on the cheek. "When are you going to leave?"

"Now, actually. I want to get there early. I need to make certain that everything is functioning. The last thing I need is a technical **mishap** to spoil the evening," the king said.

When the king arrived, he was greeted by the technical coordinator. "Are you ready to do a sound check, Your Majesty?" he asked.

"Most definitely. I want to make sure everything is in order," the king said.

The technical coordinator asked the king to speak into the microphone at the podium. "Shouldn't I practice the actual speech?" the king asked.

"Yes, yes, what was I thinking?" the coordinator replied. "We received your speech and it's ready to go. Give me a moment."

He left the king for fifteen minutes and came back looking incredibly anxious.

"What is it?" the king asked.

"It's the teleprompter, the machine with your notes on it. I can't find it."

"Surely you have another one to use in its place."

"We have several, Your Majesty. But I can't find any of them." He looked afraid that the king would explode. He'd heard that the king had a temper.

"Someone on your staff must have moved them. Find them!" the king said, raising his voice. After the coordinator left, he muttered to himself. "I have to have a teleprompter. It's not optional."

The king kept checking the time and was relieved when the coordinator finally reappeared. "Did you find one?" he asked hopefully. He felt sick when the coordinator shook his head. "How is this possible?" he asked, beginning to feel out of control.

The coordinator **cowered**, waiting to be yelled at. But the king stopped himself. "Wait. It's not your fault. I know that." He sighed. "This is more than likely the Gremlin's doing."

★ ★ ★ ★ ★ ★ ★ ★ ★

cowered – *crouched*

★ ★ ★ ★ ★ ★ ★ ★ ★

"I'm really sorry," the coordinator said. "I don't know how the teleprompters could have been misplaced."

"There's no telling how he managed to swipe them," the king said.

When the king arrived in his bedchamber at home, the queen was shocked to see him. She was holding up a dress she thought of wearing but immediately put it down. "What's wrong? Why are you home?" she asked. She was worried he was ill and felt his forehead.

"I'm not sick, dear. Although I do feel sick about what happened. There are no teleprompters. They're missing."

"Can't you find another one to use?"

"There's not time."

"Are you going to give the speech without it then?" the queen asked.

"I don't know how I can because I haven't memorized it."

"Oh," the queen said, defeated.

The couple heard a knock at the door. It was Kirk, ready to ask if his suit was acceptable for the speech. He took one look at his father's face and knew something was wrong. "What is it?" he asked.

The king explained the missing teleprompter and that he didn't have the speech memorized. He told Kirk it would be very embarrassing, but he would just have to read a printed version of the speech.

"But is that so bad?" the queen asked.

"It wouldn't be if I wasn't known for being a great speaker. I will look unprepared and unprofessional," he said, obviously disappointed.

The queen and Kirk tried to encourage him. "It will help knowing you're there with me," the king said.

Kirk left their bedchamber, saying he was going to make sure Luke and Ellen were ready. He found them and explained the problem their father had.

"Isn't there anything we can do?" Ellen asked.

Kirk was going to say no immediately but had a thought. "I don't suppose there would be anything in the guidebook that could help?"

"It's worth a try, Kirk, right?" Luke asked.

The three hurried to the library and looked up speeches in the guidebook. The entry didn't say anything about teleprompters. But there were several "see also" entries. Ellen glanced at several of them quickly until she saw the entry for keywords. "Listen to this!" she said. "There's a lot here on keywords, but I think this part could help."

Keywords
Keywords are the most important words in a sentence or piece of writing. Taking notes of just the keywords allows a writer to recreate a story or article. For example, the first line in the fairy tale "Rumpelstiltskin" reads:

Once there was a miller who was poor but had a beautiful daughter. Three of the keywords in the sentence are highlighted.

Using just the keywords in a story allows a writer to recreate it using new words and synonyms. This is good practice for beginning writers. The new sentence might be: Once upon a time, there lived an unfortunate miller who had a gorgeous daughter.

Using keywords also allows speakers to give a written speech without memorizing or reading it. The speaker can glance at the keywords and retell the main points of the speech with good eye contact.

"That's it! Father just needs to print out the keywords to his speech. He can look at them briefly and still look at the audience and the camera," Ellen said.

"I hope you're right, Ellen," Kirk said. The three of them went to find their father and see if they'd discovered a solution.

Once they saw him, Ellen explained that they had found information on keywords in the guidebook. "If I'm understanding it right, you could just have the most important words from your speech on paper. You could look at those words and still look up at people while you're speaking."

The king stared in astonishment at his daughter.

"Won't that help?" Ellen asked, worried that she didn't understand what she'd read.

"That will absolutely help!" the king said. He kissed Ellen on the cheek. "Thank you! I can't believe I didn't think of that. I've just gotten so used to having my speeches on the teleprompter. But we have no time to waste."

The king ran to his study and was out of breath. He reminded himself that he had to get back into the gym. "Screen," he called. "Please show me my speech for tonight. Every word I touch I want you to add to a new notes document."

"Yes, Your Majesty," Screen replied.

The king went over his speech quickly. He chose the words that were most likely to help him remember what he wanted to say. An assistant brought him a copy of his notes soon after he finished. The king went to find his family to tell them it was time to leave. But they were already coming to meet him. He walked quickly with them to the spaceporter. On the way, he said, "I was thinking that learning to use keywords would make a good mission for the guardians."

Kirk grinned. "Already done, Father. We had a keywords mission sent out while you were making your notes."

"That's my boy," the king said.

What's a *mishap*?

Why was the king upset when he went to practice his speech?

What is a keyword?

About the Author

Dr. Melanie Wilson was a clinical psychologist working in a Christian practice, a college instructor, freelance writer, and public speaker before she felt called to stay home and educate her children. She is a mother of six and has homeschooled for 17 years. She says it's her most fulfilling vocation.

Melanie has always been passionate about language arts and used bits and pieces of different curriculum and approaches to teach her children and friends' children. In 2014, she believed she had another calling to write the curriculum she had always wanted as a homeschooling mom — one that didn't take a lot of time, made concepts simple and memorable, and was enough fun to keep her kids motivated.

Books have been a family business since the beginning. Melanie's husband Mark has been selling library books for 30 years. Melanie and the older kids frequently pitch in to help at the annual librarians' conference. *Grammar Galaxy* is another family business that she hopes will be a great learning opportunity for their children.

When Melanie isn't busy homeschooling, visiting her oldest sons in college, or writing, she loves to play tennis with family and friends.

Melanie is also the author of *Grammar Galaxy Nebula, The Organized Homeschool Life* and *So You're Not Wonder Woman*. She is the host of The Homeschool Sanity Show podcast and author of the blog, Psychowith6.com.

About the Illustrator

Rebecca Mueller has had an interest in drawing from an early age. Rebecca quickly developed a unique style and illustrated her first books, a short series of bedtime stories with her mother, at age 9. She has since illustrated for other authors and does graphic design work for several organizations. Rebecca is currently studying at the Pierre Laclede Honors College at the University of Missouri - St. Louis and is working towards a BA in English with a minor in Studio Art - Graphic Design.

Made in United States
Orlando, FL
28 July 2022

20301841R00109